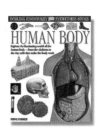 HUMAN BODY

 HURRICANE & TORNADO

 INSECT

 INVENTION

 JUNGLE

 KNIGHT

 LIGHT

 MAMMAL

 MATTER

 MEDIA & COMMUNICATION

 MEDICINE

 MEDIEVAL LIFE

 MONEY

 MUMMY

 MUSIC

 MYTHOLOGY

 NORTH AMERICAN INDIAN

 OCEAN

 OLYMPICS

 PIRATE

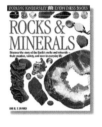 PLANT

 POND & RIVER

 PREHISTORIC LIFE

 PYRAMID

 RELIGION

 REPTILE

 RESCUE

 ROCKS & MINERALS

 SEASHORE

 SHARK

 SHELL

 SHIPWRECK

 SKELETON

 SOCCER

 SPACE EXPLORATION

 SPORTS

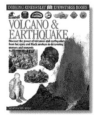 SPY

 TECHNOLOGY

 TIME & SPACE

 TITANIC

 TRAIN

 TREE

 VIKING

VOLCANO & EARTHQUAKE

WEATHER

WHALE

WILD WEST

WITCHES & MAGIC-MAKERS

WORLD WAR I

WORLD WAR II

DORLING KINDERSLEY DK EYEWITNESS BOOKS

SHARK

Sharktooth gauntlet, Kiribati, western Pacific Ocean

Copepods, which attach themselves to sharks' fins

Undulate ray

Angel shark

Model of a male great white shark

Baby dogfish

Sharktooth "brass" knuckles from the Hawaiian Islands

DK EYEWITNESS BOOKS

SHARK

Written by
MIRANDA MACQUITTY

Fossil tooth of a megalodon

Epaulette shark

Shark-shaped gold weight, from Ghana, West Africa

Sharktooth necklace from New Zealand

Swell shark

DK
Dorling Kindersley

Port
Jackson
shark

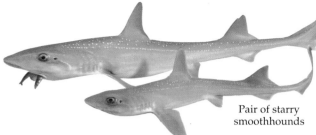

Pair of starry
smoothhounds

Leopard shark

Fossil of
Ptychodus
tooth

DK

Dorling Kindersley
LONDON, NEW YORK, AUCKLAND, DELHI, JOHANNESBURG,
MUNICH, PARIS and SYDNEY

Long spear for
catching sharks,
Nicobar Islands, India

For a full catalog, visit
DK www.dk.com

Project editor Marion Dent
Art editor Jill Plank
Managing editor Helen Parker
Managing art editor Julia Harris
Production Louise Barratt
Picture research Suzanne Williams
Special photography Frank Greenaway and Dave King
Editorial consultant Dr Geoffrey Waller
Model makers Graham High and Jeremy Hunt
Special thanks Sea Life Centres (UK)

This Eyewitness ® Book has been conceived by
Dorling Kindersley Limited and Editions Gallimard

© 1992 Dorling Kindersley Limited
This edition © 2000 Dorling Kindersley Limited
First American edition, 1992

Published in the United States by
Dorling Kindersley Publishing, Inc.
95 Madison Avenue
New York, NY 10016
4 6 8 10 9 7 5 3

Shark rattle,
Samoa, South
Pacific

Rayskin-
covered
scabbard used
by Ashanti
tribe, Ghana,
West Africa

Dorling Kindersley books are available at special discounts for bulk purchases for
sales promotions or premiums. Special editions, including personalized covers,
excerpts of existing guides, and corporate imprints can be created in large
quantities for specific needs. For more information, contact Special Markets Dept.,
Dorling Kindersley Publishing, Inc., 95 Madison Ave., New York, NY 10016;
Fax: (800) 600-9098

Library of Congress Cataloging-in-Publication Data
MacQuitty, Miranda.
Shark / by Miranda MacQuitty;
special photography by Frank Greenaway and Dave King.
p. cm. — (Eyewitness Books)
Includes index.
Summary: Describes, in text and photographs, the physical
characteristics, behavior, and life cycle of various types of sharks.
1. Sharks — Juvenile literature. [1.Sharks.]
I. Greenaway, Frank, ill. II. King, Dave, ill. III. Title.
QL638.9.M25 2000 597'.31—dc20 92-4712
ISBN 0-7894-5779-2 (pb)
ISBN 0-7894-5778-4 (hc)

Color reproduction by Colourscan, Singapore
Printed in China by Toppan Printing Co. (Shenzhen) Ltd.

Contents

Model of a
great white
shark

What is a shark?

MANY PEOPLE THINK of sharks as mean and menacing, with their pointed snouts, fearsome teeth, and staring eyes. Sharks are skillful predators, but only a few are a danger to people. The 375 or so species of shark range in size from the dwarf dogshark at about 6.5 in (16 cm) long to the whale shark at over 40 ft (12 m) long, but half the species are less than 3.3 ft (1 m) long. Not all sharks are as streamlined as this spinner shark. Angel sharks have flat bodies; horn sharks are blunt-headed; and bamboo sharks are long and flexible. All sharks belong to one class of fish called Chondrichthyes, which have skeletons made of gristlelike cartilage. Sharks live in the sea, though a few live in or swim into inland waters.

STINGRAY
This puppet-show submersible is named after a close relative of the shark (pp. 8–9).

Dorsa fi

Long, pointed snout

Mouth beneath snout, as in most sharks

Gill slits – most sharks have five

Pectoral fin – helps lift shark in water as it swims along, plus acts as a brake, but the fin cannot be folded up like those of a bony fish

Side view of a spinner shark – a classic shark shape

Sawsharks

Bramble sharks

Dogfish sharks

Rough sharks

Hammerhead sharks

Requiem sharks

Weasel sharks

Smoothhounds

Barbeled houndshark

False cat shark

Finback cat sharks

Cat sharks

Long snout

Rounded body

Flat body

Mouth below snout

Mouth at end of snout

Angel sharks

No anal fin

Short snout

Frill shark

Cow sharks

Anal fin

6–7 gill slits, 1 dorsal fin

5 gill slits, 2 dorsal fins

Fin spines

No fin spines

Horn sharks

Collared carpet sharks

Blind sharks

Wobbegongs

Bamboo sharks

Whale sha

Nurse shar

Zebra sha

Mouth in front of eyes

Mouth behind eyes

Thresher shar

Mackerel shar

Basking sha

Megamouth shar

Crocodile sha

Goblin shar

Sand tige

Nictitating eyelid; spiral or scroll intestinal valve in gut

No nictitating eyelid; ring intestinal valve in gut

Classification of living sharks

There are about 375 species of shark which can be placed in eight groups, or orders, according to the presence or absence of certain external or internal characteristics, such as anal fins, fin spines, shape of the valve in the gut, and so on. When classifying any group of animals, scientists usually try to figure out which are more closely related to each other and put those in a group together. But it is not always possible to sort out all the relationships, so some may be grouped together just for convenience. Classification may change when new sharks are discovered or when further studies reveal new relationships.

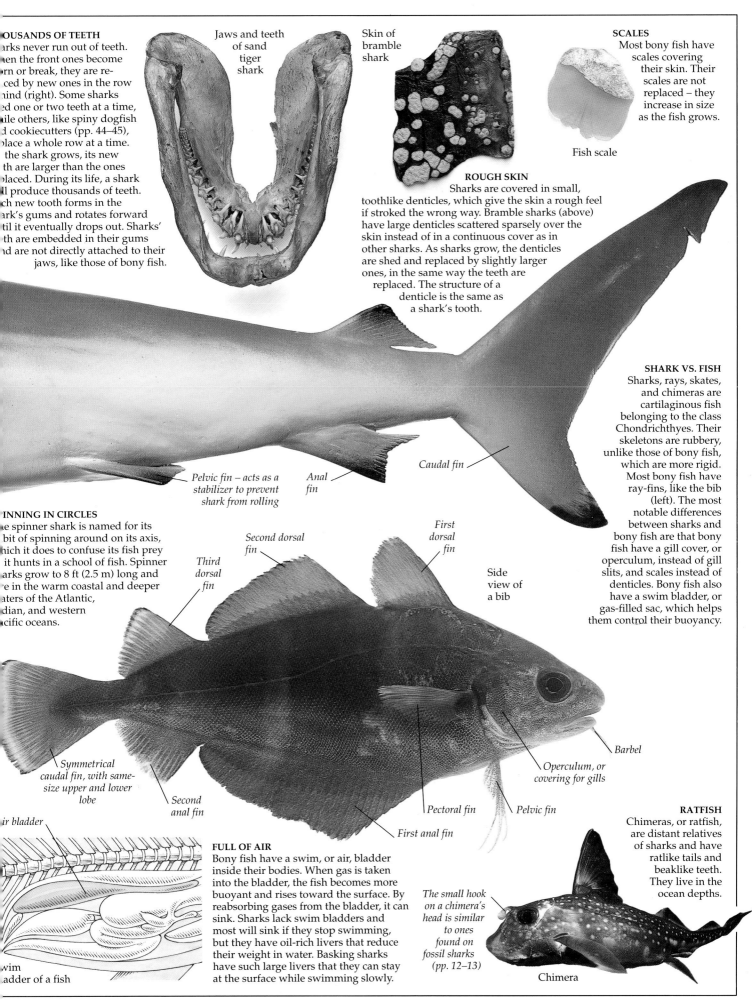

THOUSANDS OF TEETH

[Sh]arks never run out of teeth. [Wh]en the front ones become [wo]rn or break, they are re-[pla]ced by new ones in the row [beh]ind (right). Some sharks [she]d one or two teeth at a time, [wh]ile others, like spiny dogfish [an]d cookiecutters (pp. 44–45), [rep]lace a whole row at a time. [As] the shark grows, its new [tee]th are larger than the ones [rep]laced. During its life, a shark [wil]l produce thousands of teeth. [Ea]ch new tooth forms in the [sha]rk's gums and rotates forward [un]til it eventually drops out. Sharks' [tee]th are embedded in their gums [an]d are not directly attached to their jaws, like those of bony fish.

Jaws and teeth of sand tiger shark

Skin of bramble shark

SCALES

Most bony fish have scales covering their skin. Their scales are not replaced – they increase in size as the fish grows.

Fish scale

ROUGH SKIN

Sharks are covered in small, toothlike denticles, which give the skin a rough feel if stroked the wrong way. Bramble sharks (above) have large denticles scattered sparsely over the skin instead of in a continuous cover as in other sharks. As sharks grow, the denticles are shed and replaced by slightly larger ones, in the same way the teeth are replaced. The structure of a denticle is the same as a shark's tooth.

SHARK VS. FISH

Sharks, rays, skates, and chimeras are cartilaginous fish belonging to the class Chondrichthyes. Their skeletons are rubbery, unlike those of bony fish, which are more rigid. Most bony fish have ray-fins, like the bib (left). The most notable differences between sharks and bony fish are that bony fish have a gill cover, or operculum, instead of gill slits, and scales instead of denticles. Bony fish also have a swim bladder, or gas-filled sac, which helps them control their buoyancy.

Pelvic fin – acts as a stabilizer to prevent shark from rolling

Anal fin

Caudal fin

[SP]INNING IN CIRCLES

[Th]e spinner shark is named for its [ha]bit of spinning around on its axis, [wh]ich it does to confuse its fish prey [as] it hunts in a school of fish. Spinner [sh]arks grow to 8 ft (2.5 m) long and [liv]e in the warm coastal and deeper [wa]ters of the Atlantic, [In]dian, and western [Pa]cific oceans.

Third dorsal fin

Second dorsal fin

First dorsal fin

Side view of a bib

Symmetrical caudal fin, with same-size upper and lower lobe

Second anal fin

Barbel

Operculum, or covering for gills

Pectoral fin

Pelvic fin

First anal fin

[Sw]im [bl]adder

FULL OF AIR

Bony fish have a swim, or air, bladder inside their bodies. When gas is taken into the bladder, the fish becomes more buoyant and rises toward the surface. By reabsorbing gases from the bladder, it can sink. Sharks lack swim bladders and most will sink if they stop swimming, but they have oil-rich livers that reduce their weight in water. Basking sharks have such large livers that they can stay at the surface while swimming slowly.

[Sw]im [bl]adder of a fish

The small hook on a chimera's head is similar to ones found on fossil sharks (pp. 12–13)

RATFISH

Chimeras, or ratfish, are distant relatives of sharks and have ratlike tails and beaklike teeth. They live in the ocean depths.

Chimera

Close relatives

A GRACEFUL MANTA RAY SWIMMING ALONG with slow beats of it huge wings looks nothing like a sleek reef shark. Yet rays and their cousins – skates, guitarfish, and sawfish – all belong to the same group as sharks, called elasmobranchs. Members of this group have cartilaginous skeletons, which are flexible like rubber, and gill slits instead of the flaplike opercula, or gill covers, found in bony fish and chimeras (pp. 6–7). All rays have winglike pectoral fins running the length of the head and body, and gill slits on their undersides. Most rays live on the seabed, where they feed on fish, shellfish, and worms.

THE MIGHTY MANTA
Manta rays, or devilfish, have enormous pectoral fins (wings) that measure up to 23 ft (7 m) across. This magnificent female specimen, caught off the New Jersey coast, weighed almost 2,860 lb (1,300 kg). These harmless filter feeders use the large lobes on their heads to channel plankton into their wide mouths.

Starry ray

Spines increase in size along body from minute at snout to larger at tip of tail

Blonde ray

Spotted ray

SPOT TI DIFFERENC
There is a gre variety amo rays in the patte on their upper sid The pattern helps camouflage them wh they rest on the seabe The spots on the blon ray go right to the edge its pectoral fins; those on t spotted ray do not. The unde sides of rays are usually whi

Second dorsal fin

First dorsal fin

Painted ray

Spines along back for extra protection against predators

RAY OR SKATE?
Thornback ray is often sold as edible skate, but common skate actually grows to twice the thornback's size, reaching 6.5 ft (2 m) long.

Guitarfish

STRANGE RAYS
Guitarfish (50 species) and sawfish (six species) belong to the same group as rays. Guitarfish live mostly in warmer seas, but sawfish are also found in rivers and lakes. Sawfish look like sawsharks but do not have the two long barbels in the middle of their "saws," and their gill slits are on the undersides of their bodies, not on the sides of their heads. Saw-fish and sawsharks use their saws for feeding and defending themselves.

Sawfish

BABY RAY
This one-month old spotted baby ray will take eight years before it matures and is able to reproduce.

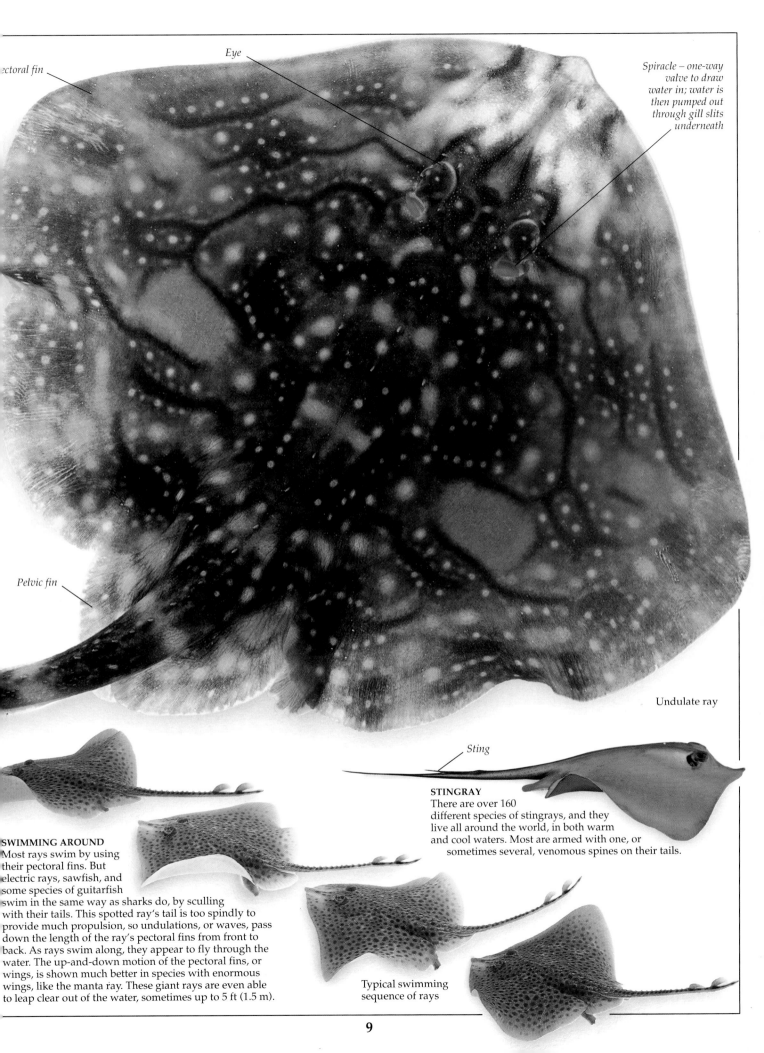

Pectoral fin

Eye

Spiracle – one-way valve to draw water in; water is then pumped out through gill slits underneath

Pelvic fin

Undulate ray

Sting

STINGRAY
There are over 160 different species of stingrays, and they live all around the world, in both warm and cool waters. Most are armed with one, or sometimes several, venomous spines on their tails.

SWIMMING AROUND
Most rays swim by using their pectoral fins. But electric rays, sawfish, and some species of guitarfish swim in the same way as sharks do, by sculling with their tails. This spotted ray's tail is too spindly to provide much propulsion, so undulations, or waves, pass down the length of the ray's pectoral fins from front to back. As rays swim along, they appear to fly through the water. The up-and-down motion of the pectoral fins, or wings, is shown much better in species with enormous wings, like the manta ray. These giant rays are even able to leap clear out of the water, sometimes up to 5 ft (1.5 m).

Typical swimming sequence of rays

Inside a shark

Packaged neatly inside this spinner shark's body are all the organs that keep it alive. To breathe, sharks have gills that absorb oxygen from the water and release carbon dioxide back into it. These gases are transported to and from the gills by the blood. The heart pumps the blood around the body, delivering oxygen and nutrients while taking away carbon dioxide and other wastes. To get energy for all their activities, including growth and repair, sharks need to eat. Food passes from the mouth into the digestive system, which is like a large tube. From the mouth the food goes down the gullet into the stomach, where digestion begins, and then into the intestine where digested food is absorbed. Indigestible wastes collect in the rectum to be passed out of the body. Digested food is further processed in the large liver. Kidneys remove wastes from the blood and regulate blood concentration. Large muscles in the body wall keep the shark swimming, and the skeleton and skin provide support. The brain coordinates the shark's actions with signals or instructions passed back and forth along the spinal cord. Finally, sharks, like all animals, cannot live forever and must reproduce to carry on the species. Female sharks have ovaries that produce eggs, and males produce sperm from their testes. When sperm meets egg, a new life begins.

DANGER BELOW
Sharks have been known to attack people coming down into water, as this Australian parachutist will soon discover.

Paired kidneys regulate waste products to keep the concentration of body fluids just above that of seawater, or sharks will dehydrate

Segmented swimming muscles contract alternately, sending a wave motion from head to tail

Model of female spinner shark, showing internal anatomy

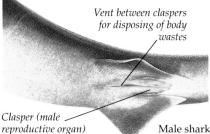

Vent between claspers for disposing of body wastes

Clasper (male reproductive organ)

Male shark

Female shark (claspers absent)

Cloaca (opening for reproduction, and vent for waste disposal)

MALE OR FEMALE
All male sharks have a pair of claspers that are formed from the inner edge of their pelvic fins. During mating, one of the claspers is rotated forward and inserted into the female's body opening, or cloaca. Sperm is pumped down a groove in the clasper into the female, so fertilization of her eggs takes place inside her body.

Rectal gland (third kidney) passes excess salt out of the body through the vent

Scroll valve in intestine, or gut; some sharks have spiral or ring valves

Left lobe of large liver

Caudal fin

Vertebral column

Cartilaginous rod

Dermal filament

ALL IN THE TAIL
Sharks have a vertebral column, or backbone, that extends into the upper lobe of their caudal fin, or tail. This type of caudal fin is called a heterocercal tail, as opposed to those in most bony fish, where the upper lobe does not contain an extension of the upper vertebral column. Cartilaginous rods and dermal filaments help to strengthen the shark's tail.

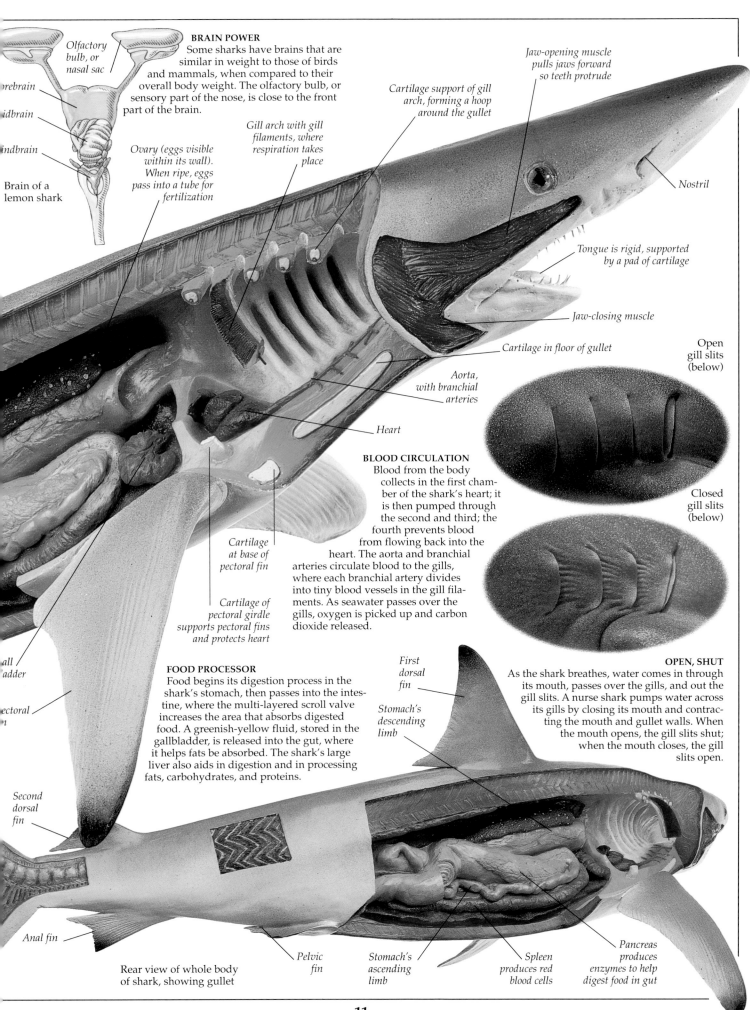

BRAIN POWER
Some sharks have brains that are similar in weight to those of birds and mammals, when compared to their overall body weight. The olfactory bulb, or sensory part of the nose, is close to the front part of the brain.

Olfactory bulb, or nasal sac

orebrain

idbrain

indbrain

Brain of a lemon shark

Ovary (eggs visible within its wall). When ripe, eggs pass into a tube for fertilization

Gill arch with gill filaments, where respiration takes place

Cartilage support of gill arch, forming a hoop around the gullet

Jaw-opening muscle pulls jaws forward so teeth protrude

Nostril

Tongue is rigid, supported by a pad of cartilage

Jaw-closing muscle

Cartilage in floor of gullet

Aorta, with branchial arteries

Heart

Open gill slits (below)

BLOOD CIRCULATION
Blood from the body collects in the first chamber of the shark's heart; it is then pumped through the second and third; the fourth prevents blood from flowing back into the heart. The aorta and branchial arteries circulate blood to the gills, where each branchial artery divides into tiny blood vessels in the gill filaments. As seawater passes over the gills, oxygen is picked up and carbon dioxide released.

Closed gill slits (below)

Cartilage at base of pectoral fin

Cartilage of pectoral girdle supports pectoral fins and protects heart

all adder

ectoral n

FOOD PROCESSOR
Food begins its digestion process in the shark's stomach, then passes into the intestine, where the multi-layered scroll valve increases the area that absorbs digested food. A greenish-yellow fluid, stored in the gallbladder, is released into the gut, where it helps fats be absorbed. The shark's large liver also aids in digestion and in processing fats, carbohydrates, and proteins.

First dorsal fin

Stomach's descending limb

OPEN, SHUT
As the shark breathes, water comes in through its mouth, passes over the gills, and out the gill slits. A nurse shark pumps water across its gills by closing its mouth and contracting the mouth and gullet walls. When the mouth opens, the gill slits shut; when the mouth closes, the gill slits open.

Second dorsal fin

Anal fin

Rear view of whole body of shark, showing gullet

Pelvic fin

Stomach's ascending limb

Spleen produces red blood cells

Pancreas produces enzymes to help digest food in gut

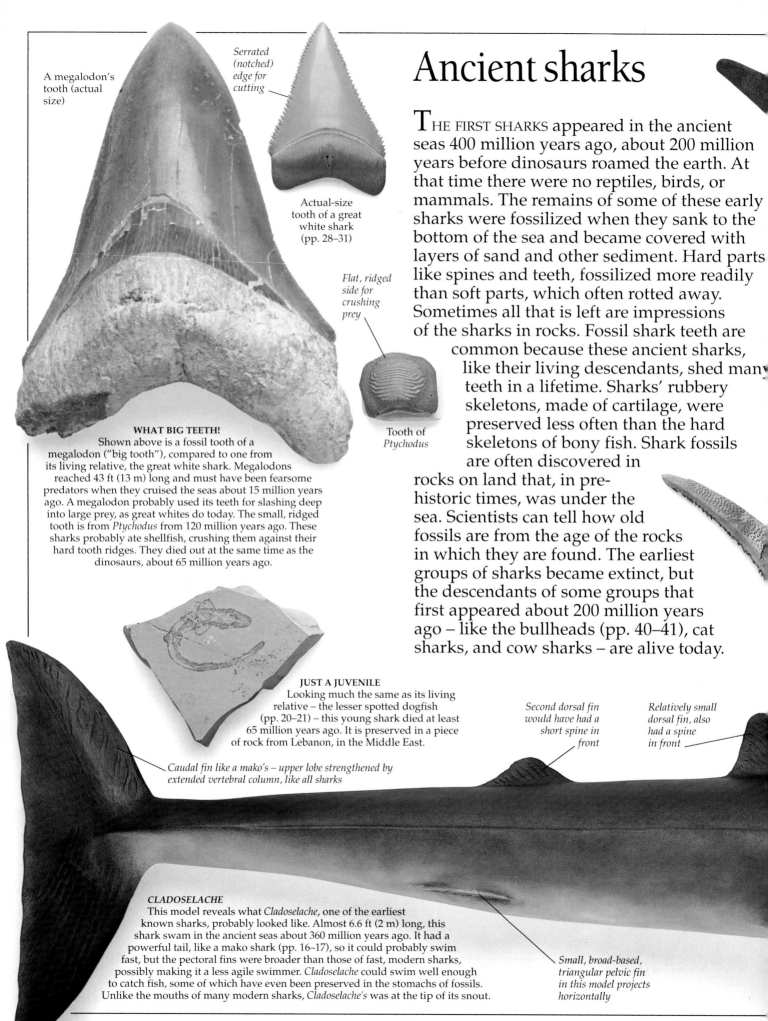

A megalodon's tooth (actual size)

Serrated (notched) edge for cutting

Actual-size tooth of a great white shark (pp. 28–31)

Flat, ridged side for crushing prey

Tooth of *Ptychodus*

Ancient sharks

THE FIRST SHARKS appeared in the ancient seas 400 million years ago, about 200 million years before dinosaurs roamed the earth. At that time there were no reptiles, birds, or mammals. The remains of some of these early sharks were fossilized when they sank to the bottom of the sea and became covered with layers of sand and other sediment. Hard parts like spines and teeth, fossilized more readily than soft parts, which often rotted away. Sometimes all that is left are impressions of the sharks in rocks. Fossil shark teeth are common because these ancient sharks, like their living descendants, shed many teeth in a lifetime. Sharks' rubbery skeletons, made of cartilage, were preserved less often than the hard skeletons of bony fish. Shark fossils are often discovered in rocks on land that, in pre-historic times, was under the sea. Scientists can tell how old fossils are from the age of the rocks in which they are found. The earliest groups of sharks became extinct, but the descendants of some groups that first appeared about 200 million years ago – like the bullheads (pp. 40–41), cat sharks, and cow sharks – are alive today.

WHAT BIG TEETH!
Shown above is a fossil tooth of a megalodon ("big tooth"), compared to one from its living relative, the great white shark. Megalodons reached 43 ft (13 m) long and must have been fearsome predators when they cruised the seas about 15 million years ago. A megalodon probably used its teeth for slashing deep into large prey, as great whites do today. The small, ridged tooth is from *Ptychodus* from 120 million years ago. These sharks probably ate shellfish, crushing them against their hard tooth ridges. They died out at the same time as the dinosaurs, about 65 million years ago.

JUST A JUVENILE
Looking much the same as its living relative – the lesser spotted dogfish (pp. 20–21) – this young shark died at least 65 million years ago. It is preserved in a piece of rock from Lebanon, in the Middle East.

Second dorsal fin would have had a short spine in front

Relatively small dorsal fin, also had a spine in front

Caudal fin like a mako's – upper lobe strengthened by extended vertebral column, like all sharks

CLADOSELACHE
This model reveals what *Cladoselache*, one of the earliest known sharks, probably looked like. Almost 6.6 ft (2 m) long, this shark swam in the ancient seas about 360 million years ago. It had a powerful tail, like a mako shark (pp. 16–17), so it could probably swim fast, but the pectoral fins were broader than those of fast, modern sharks, possibly making it a less agile swimmer. *Cladoselache* could swim well enough to catch fish, some of which have even been preserved in the stomachs of fossils. Unlike the mouths of many modern sharks, *Cladoselache*'s was at the tip of its snout.

Small, broad-based, triangular pelvic fin in this model projects horizontally

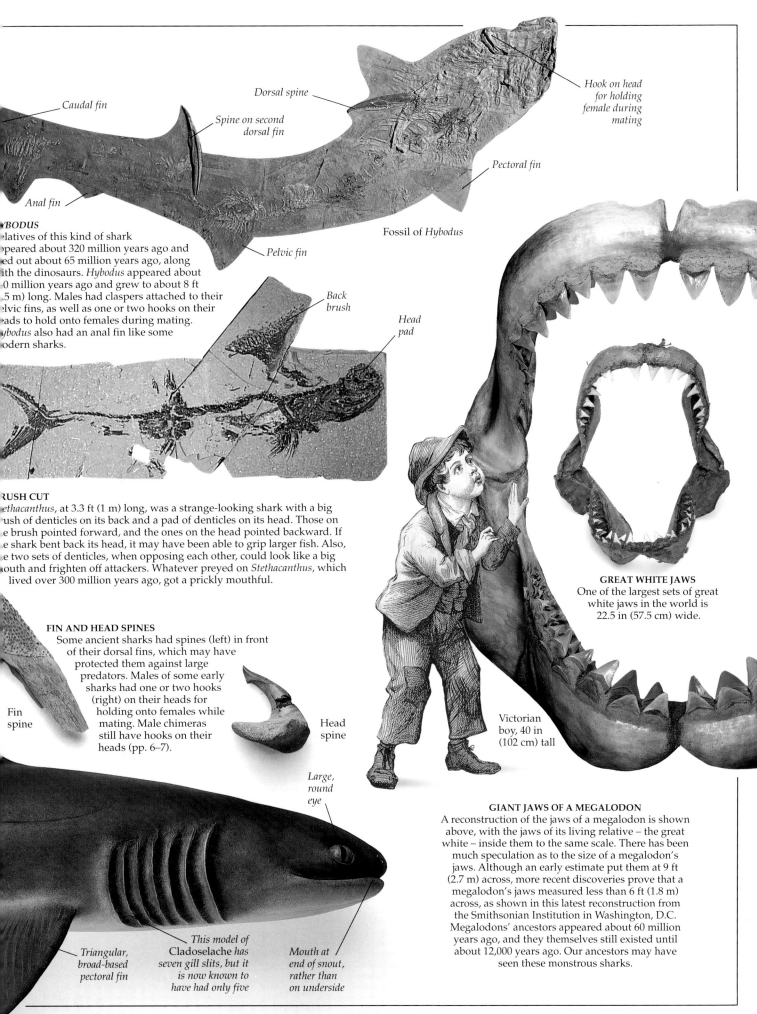

Caudal fin

Dorsal spine

Spine on second
dorsal fin

Hook on head
for holding
female during
mating

Pectoral fin

Anal fin

Fossil of *Hybodus*

Pelvic fin

YBODUS

latives of this kind of shark
ppeared about 320 million years ago and
ed out about 65 million years ago, along
ith the dinosaurs. *Hybodus* appeared about
0 million years ago and grew to about 8 ft
.5 m) long. Males had claspers attached to their
elvic fins, as well as one or two hooks on their
ads to hold onto females during mating.
ybodus also had an anal fin like some
odern sharks.

Back
brush

Head
pad

RUSH CUT

ethacanthus*, at 3.3 ft (1 m) long, was a strange-looking shark with a big
ush of denticles on its back and a pad of denticles on its head. Those on
e brush pointed forward, and the ones on the head pointed backward. If
e shark bent back its head, it may have been able to grip larger fish. Also,
e two sets of denticles, when opposing each other, could look like a big
outh and frighten off attackers. Whatever preyed on *Stethacanthus*, which
lived over 300 million years ago, got a prickly mouthful.

GREAT WHITE JAWS
One of the largest sets of great
white jaws in the world is
22.5 in (57.5 cm) wide.

FIN AND HEAD SPINES
Some ancient sharks had spines (left) in front
of their dorsal fins, which may have
protected them against large
predators. Males of some early
sharks had one or two hooks
(right) on their heads for
holding onto females while
mating. Male chimeras
still have hooks on their
heads (pp. 6–7).

Fin
spine

Head
spine

Large,
round
eye

Victorian
boy, 40 in
(102 cm) tall

GIANT JAWS OF A MEGALODON
A reconstruction of the jaws of a megalodon is shown
above, with the jaws of its living relative – the great
white – inside them to the same scale. There has been
much speculation as to the size of a megalodon's
jaws. Although an early estimate put them at 9 ft
(2.7 m) across, more recent discoveries prove that a
megalodon's jaws measured less than 6 ft (1.8 m)
across, as shown in this latest reconstruction from
the Smithsonian Institution in Washington, D.C.
Megalodons' ancestors appeared about 60 million
years ago, and they themselves still existed until
about 12,000 years ago. Our ancestors may have
seen these monstrous sharks.

Triangular,
broad-based
pectoral fin

This model of
Cladoselache has
seven gill slits, but it
is now known to
have had only five

Mouth at
end of snout,
rather than
on underside

Amazing grace

SHARKS ARE GRACEFUL swimmers. They propel themselves through the water by beating their tails from side to side. The pectoral fins are held out from the body, and as water flows over them, lift is generated to keep the shark from sinking. Further lift is produced by the upper lobe of the tail, which tends to push the head down, so that the shark can swim level. Shark fins are not nearly as flexible as those of bony fish, but small changes to the angle at which the fins are held control whether the shark goes up, down, left, or right. Pectoral fins are also used for braking. Some sharks that live on the seabed, such as horn sharks (pp. 40–41) and epaulette sharks, can use their pectoral fins to crawl along the bottom. Unlike bony fish, sharks cannot move their pectoral fins like paddles so are unable to swim backward or hover in the water. They also lack a swim bladder, which acts as a buoyancy aid in bony fish. However, sharks do have an oil-rich liver (pp. 10–11), which helps reduce their weight in water.

THE THREE GRACES
According to Greek mythology, these three daughters of Zeus were the goddesses of grace and beauty.

TAIL END
Undulations, or S-shaped waves, pass down a shark's body as it moves forward (above). The tail bends more than the rest of the body, producing a forward thrust.

STARRY SMOOTHHOUND
The denticles on a shark's skin align in the direction of travel, helping to reduce drag. These denticles may trap a film of water, which would help sharks move more easily through the water.

CRUISING
With pectoral fins held straight out from its sides, the starry smoothhound (right) keeps swimming at the same level. The two dorsal fins keep the shark from rolling, and its tail gives a forward thrust.

14

One-year-old
leopard shark,
15 in (38 cm) long

SEE HOW IT BENDS
Leopard sharks (above) have flexible
bodies, so they can turn around
in small spaces. Like their close
relatives, the smoothhounds, leopard
sharks spend much of their time cruising
close to the bottom and also resting on the seabed.

A LITTLE LIFT GOES A LONG WAY
The large pectoral fins of the starry smoothhound (left) are similar
to an airplane's wings, because they provide lift to keep the shark from
sinking. When tilted they can also act as brakes, like the flaps on the
wings of an airplane, which are raised on landing. Submarines have
horizontal fins, called hydrofoils, which lift them upward like those
of a shark. Just like a hydrofoil, the leading (or front) edge of a shark's
pectoral fin is rounded and the trailing (or rear) edge is thin, so water
flows over it more easily. The pointed snout and tapered body are
streamlined and give little resistance to the water.

FULL STEAM AHEAD
A great white shark
(above) usually cruises
at about 1.8 mph
(3 kph). Its bulky body
hardly moves at all,
while its tail beats from
side to side. When
closing in on a kill, the
great white puts on an
impressive burst of
speed of up to 15 mph
(25 kph).

BIG SURPRISE!
Great whites can bend
their bodies but are
not nearly as flexible
as smaller sharks.
They have to surprise
their prey rather than
out-maneuver them.

15

Continued on next page

Tails and more tails

The shape of a shark's tail suits its way of life. Many sharks have tail fins with an upper lobe that is larger than the lower; as the tail swings from side to side, this larger lobe produces lift, which tends to push the head down. This is compensated for by lift from the pectoral fins, which keeps the shark from sinking to the bottom. In fast sharks, like the mako and great white, these two lobes are almost equal in size. Lift may also come from the base of the tail, which in the mako has small, horizontal keels (ridges). The extra height of these more symmetrically shaped tails gives a more powerful thrust. Slow bottom-dwellers, like the nurse shark, have less powerful tails, and their swimming motion is more eel-like, with obvious waves passing down to their tails.

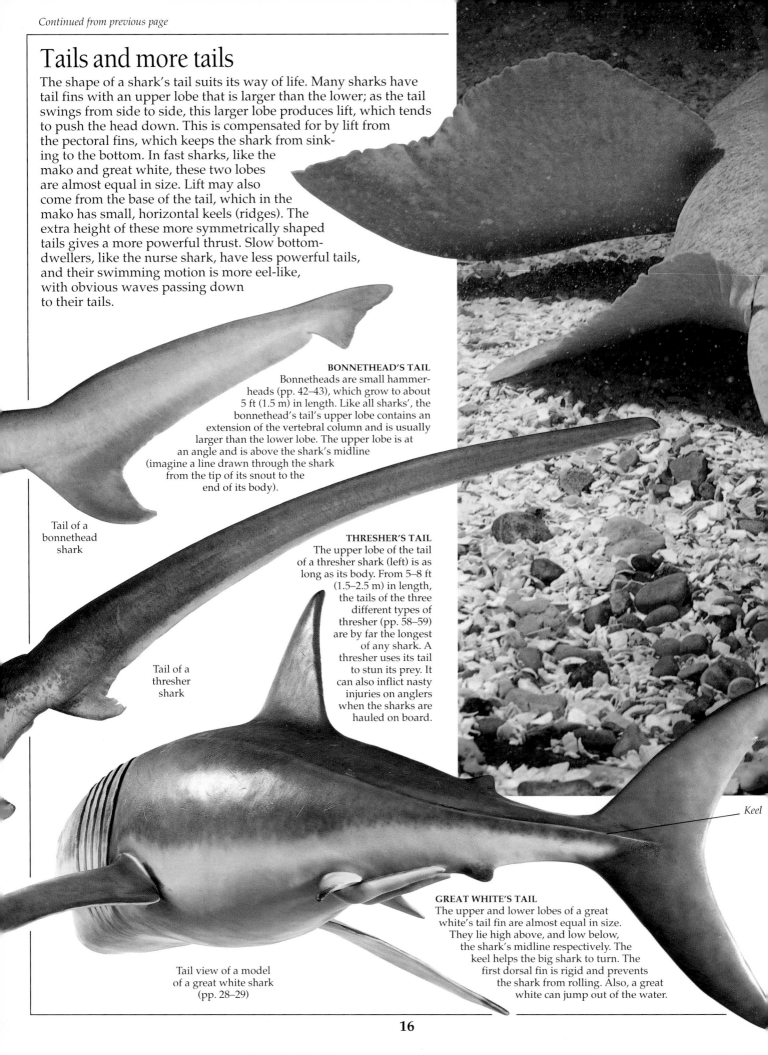

BONNETHEAD'S TAIL
Bonnetheads are small hammer-heads (pp. 42–43), which grow to about 5 ft (1.5 m) in length. Like all sharks', the bonnethead's tail's upper lobe contains an extension of the vertebral column and is usually larger than the lower lobe. The upper lobe is at an angle and is above the shark's midline (imagine a line drawn through the shark from the tip of its snout to the end of its body).

Tail of a bonnethead shark

Tail of a thresher shark

THRESHER'S TAIL
The upper lobe of the tail of a thresher shark (left) is as long as its body. From 5–8 ft (1.5–2.5 m) in length, the tails of the three different types of thresher (pp. 58–59) are by far the longest of any shark. A thresher uses its tail to stun its prey. It can also inflict nasty injuries on anglers when the sharks are hauled on board.

Keel

Tail view of a model of a great white shark (pp. 28–29)

GREAT WHITE'S TAIL
The upper and lower lobes of a great white's tail fin are almost equal in size. They lie high above, and low below, the shark's midline respectively. The keel helps the big shark to turn. The first dorsal fin is rigid and prevents the shark from rolling. Also, a great white can jump out of the water.

HEAVENLY TAKEOFF
To lift its huge body off the seabed, the angel shark beats its tail back and forth while tipping its large pectoral and pelvic fins for maximum lift. Once off the seabed, angels propel themselves forward by sculling with their tails, but they do not undulate, or wave, their pectoral fins like rays.

MIDAIR MAKO
Makos (pp. 26–27) are probably the fastest sharks in the sea, reaching speeds estimated to be 20 mph (32 kph) for a few moments. When caught on an angler's line, they leap clear of the surface in an effort to escape (above). Their tails are the same shape as another fast fish, the tuna, and like tunas they have keels along the base of their tails, which may give them more maneuverability, and perhaps provide some lift. They are active predators, pursuing mainly fish.

SWELL TAIL
Smaller than nurse sharks, at 3.3 ft (1 m) long, swell sharks (right) are sluggish animals, spending the day resting on the seabed and at night swimming close to the bottom. Their tails are set barely above their midlines.

HORN SHARK'S TAIL
The lower lobe of the horn shark's tail (pp. 40–41) is more developed than the swell shark's. The tail of this 3.3-ft (1-m) shark is also at a low angle to its midline, and it is a slow swimmer.

Lower lobe of angel shark's tail fin (pp. 36–37) is longer than upper lobe

**...IL
...A
...JRSE
...IARK**
...urse sharks,
...10 ft (3 m)
...ng, are rather
...w swimmers
...d use their tails
...ght) for cruising
...ar the bottom.

Making sense

Blue shark's nictitating eyelid
Pore
Nostril

SHARKS HAVE THE SAME FIVE SENSES as people – they can see, hear, smell, taste, and touch. There is also a sixth sense that allows sharks to detect weak electrical signals generated by their prey. This electro-sense may also help them to navigate on their journeys in the sea. The underwater world is very different from our own. Light levels decrease with depth, and colors fade to blues. Sound travels five times faster and farther. Odors are dissolved in water, not wafted in the air. Sharks can detect vibrations made by animals moving through the water, giving them the sense called "distant touch." It is hard to find out exactly how a shark perceives its world, but studies on their behavior and how sense organs work give some idea about what it is like to be a shark.

METAL DETECTOR
Sweeping a metal detector back and forth to find buried metal objects is like the way hammerheads (pp. 42–43) hunt for fish hiding in the sand.

GOING TO ITS HEAD
Like us, a shark's major sense organs are on its head. Seen on this blue shark are the eye, nostril, and sensory pores, which detect weak electrical signals. The eye is partly covered by a third eyelid, called a nictitating (or blinking) eyelid; it protects the eye when the shark attacks prey or nears unfamiliar objects. As the shark swims along, water flows through the nostril beneath the tip of the snout, bringing a constant stream of odors.

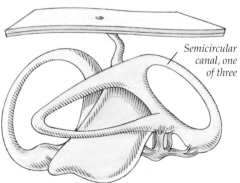

FEEDING FRENZY
When sharks are feeding on bait, they may become overexcited and snap wildly at their food. They may bite each other and even tear one another apart.

Semicircular canal, one of three

THE INNER EAR
Sharks do not have external ear flaps, but have ears inside their heads on either side of the brain case. Three semicircular canals placed at right angles to each other are like those found in the ears of all vertebrates. These canals help a shark figure out which way it has turned in the water. Receptors in the inner ear, like those in the lateral line on the skin, pick up sounds traveling through the water. Each ear has a small duct which leads to a pore on the top of the shark's head.

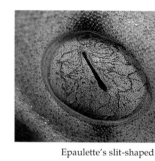
Epaulette's slit-shaped pupil

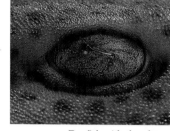
Dogfish with closed pupil

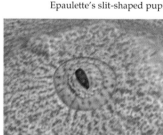
Angel shark's pupil

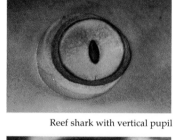
Reef shark with vertical pupil

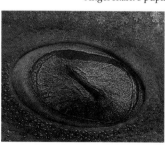
Horn shark's pupil

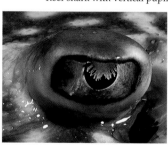
Ray with light-blocking screen

ALL KINDS OF EYES
According to how much light there is, the iris in a shark's eyes contracts or expands to alter the size of the pupil. The tapetum lucidum, a layer of cells at the back of the eye, reflects light back onto the retina, where images are focused, making maximum use of any available light. This helps sharks to see in dim light. Cats also have a tapetum, which is why their eyes reflect lights shined at them. On bright, sunny days a shark can shield its tapetum with a layer of pigment. Like a human retina, a shark retina has two types of cells – rods work in dim light and are sensitive to light changes; cones resolve details and probably allow sharks to see in color.

DISTANT TOUCH
Sharks have a lateral-line system running down each side of the body and onto the head. The lines are small canals with tiny pores beneath which are cells with minute hairs. Scattered over the body are similar hair cells called pit organs, which like the lateral lines pick up vibrations.

Lateral line

Starry smoothhound showing lateral line

18

EYES ON STALKS
Hammerheads' eyes are on the end of their head projections, giving them a good view as they swing their heads back and forth. The nostrils are widely spaced on the front of the head, helping them detect where an odor is coming from. The head projections are packed with ampullae of Lorenzini, which detect electrical signals from hidden fish.

Compass

Imaginary magnet

North-south axis

Earth's magnetic field

COMPASS SENSE
Some sharks migrate hundreds of miles and seem to know where they are going, in what to us is a featureless ocean. Scientists think sharks have compass sense to guide them. In a real compass, a magnetic needle swings around to align itself to the earth's magnetic field. The earth's magnetic field (above) is created by its core, which acts like a giant magnet. Sharks seem able to swim in one direction by sensing changes in their own electrical fields in relation to the earth's magnetic field. Corrections have to be made for speed and direction of ocean currents, which may sweep the shark off course. Sharks may also be able to navigate by detecting magnetic patterns on the seabed.

DUCKBILLED PLATYPUS
One of the few animals, apart from sharks, that has a sixth sense enabling it to detect electrical signals of its prey, is the duckbilled platypus from Australia. The platypus's electro-receptors are on the left-hand side of its bill. Platypuses live in streams, where they hunt for insects and other small creatures on the river bottom.

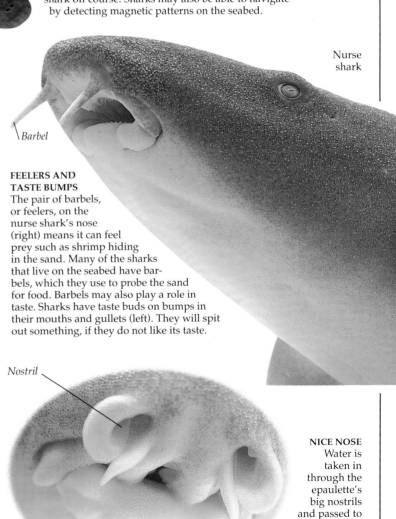

Nurse shark

Barbel

FEELERS AND TASTE BUMPS
The pair of barbels, or feelers, on the nurse shark's nose (right) means it can feel prey such as shrimp hiding in the sand. Many of the sharks that live on the seabed have barbels, which they use to probe the sand for food. Barbels may also play a role in taste. Sharks have taste buds on bumps in their mouths and gullets (left). They will spit out something, if they do not like its taste.

Nostril

SPOTTY NOSE
The spots in front of the nostrils on this sand tiger's snout are sensory pores called ampullae of Lorenzini. The deep pores are full of jelly and connect at their base to nerves; they detect weak electrical signals produced by a prey's muscles and bodily processes. Sometimes sharks are confused by electrical signals given off by metal, so they will bite shark cages (pp. 52–53).

Snout of an epaulette shark

NICE NOSE
Water is taken in through the epaulette's big nostrils and passed to a nasal sac where odors are smelled. Sharks can detect very weak odors – as little as one drop of fish extract diluted over a million times.

19

Reproduction and laying eggs

FOR SOME SHARKS, finding a mate means a long swim, because males and females often live in different parts of the ocean. When they meet, the male chases the female, biting her to encourage her to mate. He inserts one of his claspers (extensions of his pelvic fin) into her cloaca, or body opening (pp. 10–11). Seawater already drawn into a sac in the male's body is then squirted into a groove in his clasper. This water flushes sperm into her cloaca. In this way, the sperm fertilizes the female's eggs inside her body. In contrast, in bony fish, fertilization occurs outside the body, with sperm and eggs being shed into the water. Some female sharks can store sperm until they are ready to reproduce, so fertilization may not happen immediately. Most sharks give birth to live young (pp. 22–23), but some reproduce by laying eggs. The fertilized eggs are encased in a leathery shell and deposited by the female on the seabed, where the embryos, or developing shark pups, grow until they are ready to hatch. These sharks are oviparous, which means their young hatch from an egg laid outside the mother – just like birds and bony fish.

SPIRAL EGG
A horn shark wedge its spiral-shaped egg case into rocks, protec ing it from predators

CAT'S EGG
The cat shark's egg case is firmly anchore onto anything growin on the seabed. Shark eggs are large and we protected; because of this they stand a bette chance of survival tha the masses of small eggs laid by bony fish

MERMAIDS
Mermaids are mythical sea creatures with a woman's body and a fish's tail. Since ancient times, sailors have made up stories about mermaids. The empty egg cases of dogfish and rays that wash up on the seashore are called mermaids' purses.

CATCH ME IF YOU CAN
This male whitetip reef shark is pursuing a female in the hope that she will mate with him. He may be attracted by her smell.

LOVE BITES
When a male whitetip reef shark gets close to a female (right), he bites her to arouse her interest. He will also grab her pectoral fin in his jaws to keep her close to him during mating. Very little is known of the mating habits of other large sharks.

THICK SKIN
Some female sharks, like this blue shark, have much thicker skin than males, which prevents serious injury during courtship. Most "love bites" are only skin deep and heal in a few weeks.

MATING SHARKS
People rarely see sharks mating in the wild, or even in aquar- iums. From a few obser- vations, it seems that larger sharks mate side to side. Whitetip reef sharks (left) mate side to side and may pivot on their heads. The male of smaller sharks, such as dogfish (or cat sharks), is more flexible and wraps himself around the female when mating.

Tendril

DOGFISH EGGS
Every year female small spotted cat sharks, also known as lesser spotted dogfish, lay about 20 eggs in seaweed. The developing dogfish lie safe inside their egg cases. At first the egg cases are soft, but soon they harden in the seawater. The tendrils at the corners of the egg capsules anchor them to seaweed to prevent them being swept away by currents. Embryos take about eight to nine months to develop before they are ready to hatch. During this time each embryo gets its nourishment from its large yolk sac.

Dogfish embryo

Yolk sac

Pair of dogfish egg cases

Pair of
ten-day-old dogfish

Cream-colored underside

DOGFISH PUPS
These young dogfish are only ten days old. They are only 4 in (10 cm) long, and they look like small versions of their parents. Shark pups are generally much larger and more developed than young of bony fish. Soon after hatching, the young dogfish start to feed on small creatures like shrimp. It will be ten years before they reach maturity and start to breed. When fully grown, dogfish are about 3 ft (1 m) long.

ONE-MONTH-OLD SWELL SHARK EMBRYO
Swell sharks live on the eastern side of the Pacific
ean in shallow coastal waters. They are called swell
arks because when threatened they wedge themselves
o a rocky crevice by gulping in mouthfuls of
ter. If taken out of the water, a swell shark can
ll swell up by taking in air. The female lays two
gs at a time, depositing them among clumps of
aweed. Each egg is protected by a leathery case.
e month after it was laid, the fertilized egg has
veloped into a tiny embryo. The large egg sac is
l of yolk, which nourishes the growing embryo.

*loring consists of
ht and dark
wn bands, with
k spots on
ark's top side*

2 EMBRYO AT THREE MONTHS
The embryo has grown much larger and already has eyes and a tail. The yolk sac is connected to the embryo's belly by a cord, and oxygen in the surrounding seawater passes through the leathery egg case so that the embryo is able to breathe.

3 SEVEN-MONTH-OLD EMBRYO
By now the embryo looks much more like a baby shark. It has a complete set of fins and is able to wriggle around inside the egg case. The two rows of spines on the baby's back will help give it a grip on the egg case as it pushes its way out. The baby shark, or pup, will hatch as soon as it has used up the rest of the yolk sac.

4 TWO-MONTH-OLD PUP
After ten months, the young swell shark (6 in, 15 cm long) has hatched from the egg case. This is a most vulnerable moment in its young life because it is so small and there are many predators. Its mottled color pattern makes it hard to see when it is hiding on the seabed. It can also wedge itself into a hiding place by swelling up.

*vo-month-old
vell shark pup*

Live young

THE MAJORITY OF SHARKS give birth to live young instead of laying eggs. Most of these sharks are ovoviviparous: that is, the embryo develops in a large, yolky egg kept inside the female's oviduct, or womblike cavity. The embryos hatch while still inside the mother, develop yet further, and then are born "again" as live baby sharks. In some ovoviviparous sharks, the first pups that develop eat any unfertilized eggs – plus their less developed brothers and sisters – in the mother's oviduct. In sand tiger sharks, for example, only one of the young cannibals survives in each side of the "womb." In viviparous (born live) sharks, such as lemon, blue, and bull sharks, each fertilized egg develops inside a separate compartment in the mother's oviduct. The unborn pup is fed via a placenta. As in humans and other mammals, the placenta acts like a sieve, allowing food and oxygen to pass from mother to baby, and waste materials from baby back to mother, through the connecting umbilical cord.

MOTHER AND BABY
Human babies need to be looked after for many years, but shark pups are not so lucky. They must fend for themselves as soon as they are born.

1

A LEMON SHARK IS BORN
(1) The tip of the pup's tail is just visible poking out of its mother's opening, or cloaca (pp. 10–11). Pregnant lemon sharks come into shallow coastal lagoons that are sheltered from the waves, to give birth. Scientists studying sharks at Bimini in the Bahamas sometimes catch female sharks for their research. (2) Here, the female has begun to give birth. (3) The scientist is acting like a midwife, and is helping the passage of the pup out of the mother's birth canal.

2

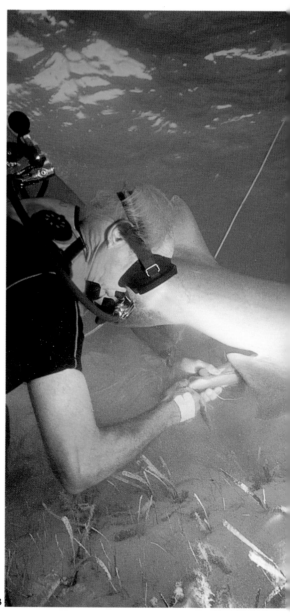

3

HAMMERHEAD PUPS
Hammerhead sharks give birth to live young that are little replicas of their parents. In one litter, up to 40 pups may be born, with their head projections bent back. In the uterus, each pup is connected to its mother by an umbilical cord.

BABY AFRICAN ELEPHANT
baby elephant takes 22 months to evelop inside its mother's womb, which is the longest gestation eriod of any mammal. The long regnancy is not surprising, since a aby elephant weighs over 220 lb 0 kg) at birth. Some sharks ave a nine-month gestation period, just like humans, though the spiny dogfish matches the elephant in taking 18 to 24 months to be born.

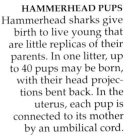

SPINY BABIES GO EASY ON THEIR MOTHERS
Giving birth is hard for any mother. Fortunately for a hedgehog mother, the spines of her babies do not poke out until after birth. The sharp spines on the dorsal fins of newborn spiny dogfish have protective coverings.

BIGEYE THRESHER PUPS
As bigeye thresher pups develop inside the uterus, they feed on bundles of un-fertilized eggs. The pups have long tails – just like their parents.

(4) The lemon shark pup, one of up to 17 pups, is still attached to its mother by the umbilical cord. She is nearly 10 ft (3 m) long, but her pups are only 24 in (60 cm)long.
(5) The pup will rest for a while on the sea-bed, then swim away, breaking the umbilical cord. (6) Now the pup faces life on its own. It must seek the cover of mangrove roots and hide from predators, such as larger sharks and barracudas. For many years it will stay in a small nursery area in the shallows of the lagoon, near where it was born. Then it will make exploratory trips out of the lagoon to the coral reefs and will gradually spend more time farther out to sea.

6

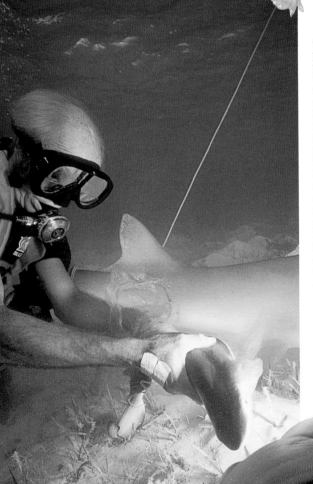

4

5

Teeth and diet

SHARKS CONTINUALLY lose their teeth. When the front ones wear out, they are replaced by new ones growing in another row behind them. An individual shark goes through thousands of teeth in a lifetime. Most animals, like elephants and seals, cannot replace their teeth, and die when the teeth wear out. As the shark grows, its new teeth are larger than the ones they replace. Sharks' teeth come in many shapes according to what kind of food they eat. Teeth like small spikes are used for gripping small prey. Serrated teeth are used for cutting. Long, curved teeth can hold slippery fish. Blunt teeth crunch up shellfish. A few species of shark, like basking and whale sharks, have tiny teeth compared to their great size. They do not use their teeth to feed; they filter food out of the water instead. Some sharks produce different-shaped teeth as they grow older.

Tiny teeth of basking shark

Gill rakers

MOUTH WIDE OPEN
Basking sharks swim along with their mouths open to catch shrimp and other small creatures called plankton that drift in the sea. The food is trapped on rows of bristles called gill rakers as the water flows through the mouth and out through the gill slits. The gill rakers are shed each year during the winter months when there is little food around. A new set of rakers grows in the spring, and then the basking sharks can start to feed again.

EPAULETTE EATING
Epaulette sharks live on coral reefs in the southwest Pacific Ocean around Australia and Papua New Guinea. They grow to about 3.3 ft (1 m) long and can crawl along the bottom using their pectoral fins. These sharks search among the shallows and tidepools for small fish, crabs, shrimps, and other small creatures to eat.

SMILE PLEASE
Swell sharks (top right) from the eastern Pacific Ocean have big mouths for their 3.3-ft (1-m) length. Armed with rows of tiny teeth, these sharks eat bony fish that rest on the seabed. Only the Port Jackson's rows of small front teeth (bottom right) are visible when its mouth is open. At the back of its jaws are strong, flat teeth for crushing shelled prey.

Epaulette eating

CRUNCHY DIET
Port Jackson sharks have small, pointed front teeth to grab their prey. The strong, flat back teeth crunch hard-shelled crabs, mussels (right), and sea urchins (below right).

Section through a Port Jackson's jaws

Mouth swell sha

Mouth Port Jacks

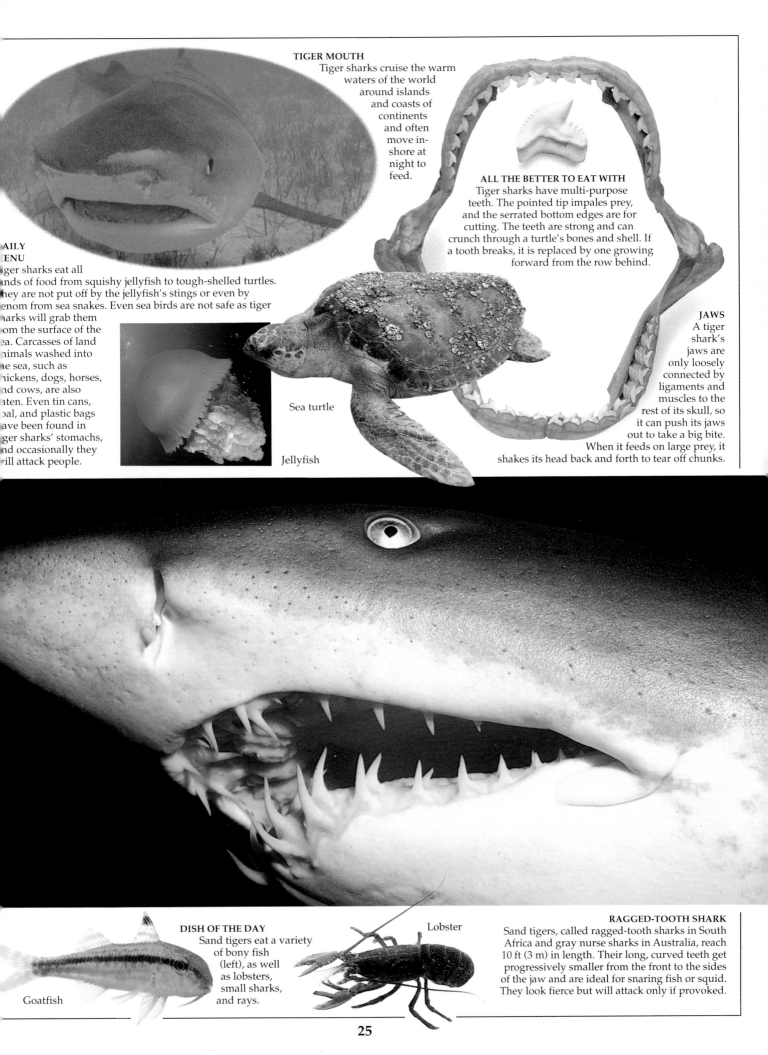

TIGER MOUTH
Tiger sharks cruise the warm waters of the world around islands and coasts of continents and often move in-shore at night to feed.

ALL THE BETTER TO EAT WITH
Tiger sharks have multi-purpose teeth. The pointed tip impales prey, and the serrated bottom edges are for cutting. The teeth are strong and can crunch through a turtle's bones and shell. If a tooth breaks, it is replaced by one growing forward from the row behind.

DAILY MENU
Tiger sharks eat all kinds of food from squishy jellyfish to tough-shelled turtles. They are not put off by the jellyfish's stings or even by venom from sea snakes. Even sea birds are not safe as tiger sharks will grab them from the surface of the sea. Carcasses of land animals washed into the sea, such as chickens, dogs, horses, and cows, are also eaten. Even tin cans, coal, and plastic bags have been found in tiger sharks' stomachs, and occasionally they will attack people.

Sea turtle

Jellyfish

JAWS
A tiger shark's jaws are only loosely connected by ligaments and muscles to the rest of its skull, so it can push its jaws out to take a big bite. When it feeds on large prey, it shakes its head back and forth to tear off chunks.

DISH OF THE DAY
Sand tigers eat a variety of bony fish (left), as well as lobsters, small sharks, and rays.

Goatfish

Lobster

RAGGED-TOOTH SHARK
Sand tigers, called ragged-tooth sharks in South Africa and gray nurse sharks in Australia, reach 10 ft (3 m) in length. Their long, curved teeth get progressively smaller from the front to the sides of the jaw and are ideal for snaring fish or squid. They look fierce but will attack only if provoked.

Friend or foe?

LIKE MOST ANIMALS, sharks have a variety of small friends and enemies that choose to live on, in, or near them. Small fish called remoras often hitch rides on sharks using suckers on their heads. Remoras help sharks stay healthy by eating the tiny shellfish called copepods that often infest sharks' fins and gills. Sometimes remoras hitch rides on the bow waves produced by a shark swimming though the water. Other kinds of fish, called pilot fish, also swim with sharks and ride their bow waves. Pilot fish probably feed off scraps left over after a shark's meal. Copepods, tapeworms, and other parasites live on or within sharks feeding off their skin, blood, or digested food. Parasites may cause a shark discomfort, but they will rarely kill it.

CLAWS
This 0.75-in-long (19-mm) copepod digs its sharp claws into a basking shark's skin. It feeds on skin secretions and blood. Basking sharks, infested by these and other parasites, become irritated. Reports tell of sharks leaping clear of the water to get rid of them.

Claw
Antenna
Head
Thoracic plate, or body section
Abdomen

BARNACLES ABOARD
This strange-looking lump is a barnacle, related to the ones found on the seashore. In the sea, the larvae, or young, of this barnacle attach themselves to dorsal fins of spurdogs or dogfish. The root, or stalk, of this 1-in-long (26-mm) barnacle has rootlets that absorb nutrients from the shark.

Soft shell
Root
Rootlet for absorbing food from shark

CLEAN TEETH
Other animals hav friends too. A bir cleans a crocodile teeth and finds son thing tasty to eat

Female   Male

CLING ONS
These small (0.5 in, 13 mm) crustaceans, or copepods, have adhesive pads to stick onto sharks' fins. They feed on skin secretions.

STREAMERS
Copepods are clinging onto the dorsal fins of this mako shark (above) and have egg cases streaming out behind them. Each case contains a stack of disk-shaped eggs. When the eggs are released, they hatch into tiny young, or larvae. These larvae drift about in the sea, passing through several stages of development before attaching themselves to a passing shark.

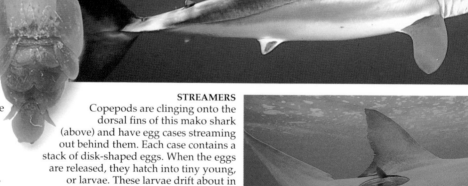

STICKIN TOGETH
Shark suckers, remoras (left), live in t world's tropical oceans. Each h a ridged sucker on the top of its he that it uses to attach itself to sharks and ra While hitching a ride, remoras often do their ho a favor by nibbling off skin parasites. They may also st scraps when the shark has a meal and even feed on the placer (pp. 40–41), when a shark gives birth to pups (abov

PILOT FISH
Young golden trevally from the Pacific Ocean swim with larger fish, including sharks. Though they are called pilot fish, they do not guide sharks and other large fish to sources of food. They just like to school with larger fish. They may also be protected from other fish that do not like to be close to sharks. Pilot fish are much too agile to be eaten themselves.

Anchor which embeds in eye's surface

Arm

Head

Trunk

Egg sac, containing thousands of eggs

Tentacle

Head

Body

MOBILE HOME
Whale sharks (top) are so big that they provide living space for large numbers of remoras. Some remoras congregate around the mouth, even swimming inside the mouth cavity and gills, where they may feed on parasites; others nestle around the cloaca on a female shark (above). Remoras get free transportation from their giant hosts, by either attaching themselves or riding the shark's bow wave.

WORMS AND MORE WORMS
Hundreds of 1-ft (30-cm) tapeworms may live in a shark's gut, where they absorb food. Segments full of eggs from their tail ends are passed into the sea; the eggs hatch when eaten by a copepod. The young worm is passed to a bony fish when the fish eats the copepod. If a shark eats the fish, the cycle begins again.

EYE SPY
This strange copepod hangs by its long arms to a Greenland shark's eye. At 1.2 in long (31 mm), the parasite makes it hard for a 20-ft (6-m) shark to see. It feeds on the eye's surface tissues, but once there, it cannot let go.

NAVIGATING
A large ship is guided into harbor by pilot boats, but sharks navigate on their own (pp. 18–19).

The great white shark

A POWERFUL PREDATOR, the great white inspires fear. This awesome shark grows to over 20 ft (6 m) long and weighs more than 2.4 tons (2.2 tonnes). It is the largest of the predatory sharks, capable of eating seals whole. The great white became famous in the *Jaws* movies, where it appears as a bloodthirsty creature intent on killing people. Attacks (pp. 48–49) on people are rare and possibly occur when a shark mistakes a person for its usual prey, the seal. Despite its fame, little is known about the great white. Scientists have yet to discover where mating and birth occur, or what the shark's age is when it reproduces or dies. No one knows how many great whites there are, but in some areas they may be on the decline.

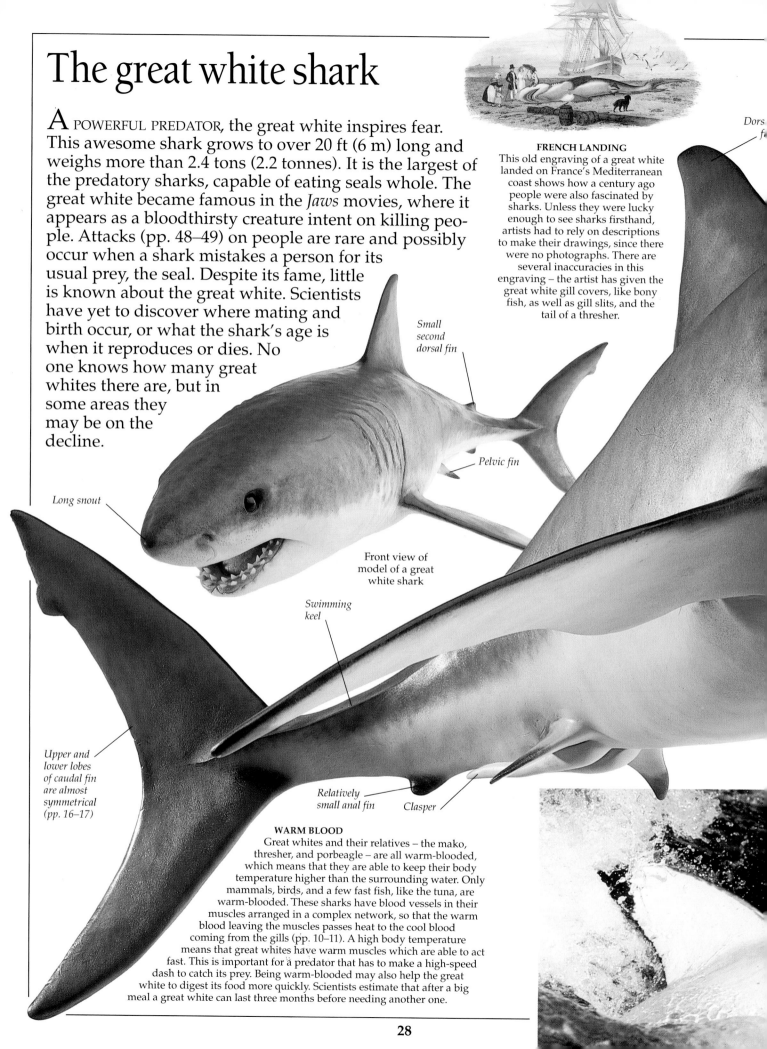

FRENCH LANDING
This old engraving of a great white landed on France's Mediterranean coast shows how a century ago people were also fascinated by sharks. Unless they were lucky enough to see sharks firsthand, artists had to rely on descriptions to make their drawings, since there were no photographs. There are several inaccuracies in this engraving – the artist has given the great white gill covers, like bony fish, as well as gill slits, and the tail of a thresher.

Dors
f

Small second dorsal fin

Pelvic fin

Long snout

Front view of model of a great white shark

Swimming keel

Upper and lower lobes of caudal fin are almost symmetrical (pp. 16–17)

Relatively small anal fin

Clasper

WARM BLOOD
Great whites and their relatives – the mako, thresher, and porbeagle – are all warm-blooded, which means that they are able to keep their body temperature higher than the surrounding water. Only mammals, birds, and a few fast fish, like the tuna, are warm-blooded. These sharks have blood vessels in their muscles arranged in a complex network, so that the warm blood leaving the muscles passes heat to the cool blood coming from the gills (pp. 10–11). A high body temperature means that great whites have warm muscles which are able to act fast. This is important for a predator that has to make a high-speed dash to catch its prey. Being warm-blooded may also help the great white to digest its food more quickly. Scientists estimate that after a big meal a great white can last three months before needing another one.

Pore, marking position of ampullae of Lorenzini – sensory organs for detecting prey's electric field (pp. 18–19)

ong gill it – one f five

Sharp, serrated (notched) teeth

WHITE DEATH
A great white's coloring makes it difficult to see in the water, so it is able to sneak up on its victims. When seen from below, a shark's white undersides blend in with a bright sky's reflection at the water's surface. This magnificent shark is sometimes called "white pointer," referring to its pointed snout which makes it more streamlined. Great whites often have scratches and scars on their snouts, which may be the result of their prey fighting back. They are also sometimes bitten by larger members of their own kind that move in to take food away from them.

Pectoral fin

ull-length side view of model of a male great white shark

TAKING THE BAIT
Scientists, filmmakers, and photographers use chum (a mixture of blood and rotting fish) and other bait to attract great whites. Great whites are among the few sharks that stick their heads out of the water before, and sometimes during, attacks on prey. As the shark takes the bait, its eyes roll back in their sockets revealing the white surface of the eyeball. This protects the more vital front part of the eye from being scratched, which may happen if the shark is attacking live prey, such as a seal armed with claws and teeth.

TAGGING A GREAT WHITE
Dr. John McCosker, an American shark scientist, tags a great white off the Australian coast (top). Sonic tags have revealed that a great white can cruise at 1.8 mph (3 kph), traveling about 120 miles (200 km) in three days (above).

29

Continued on next page

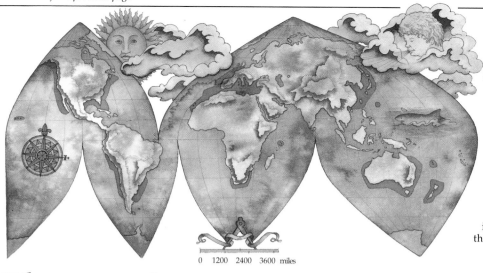

Distribution of the great white shark

BIG BITE
The great white's upper jaw protrudes forward, and its snout tips upward (right) so it can grab a chunk of meat. This shark may realize that there is no danger of its prey retaliating, because the shark's eyes face forward and are not rolled back.

What a great white eats

Great white sharks live in the cool to warm waters along the coasts of North and South America, north and south Africa, the Mediterranean, Japan, China, Korea, Australia, and New Zealand. They also occur occasionally around some islands in the mid-Pacific and Atlantic oceans. They are often seen near seal colonies, where they prey on both adults and young, but only a few sharks seem to hunt in any one area. When attacking a seal, a great white approaches unseen from below, takes a bite, then moves off for a short while. The prey soon weakens because of loss of blood and shock, and the shark can then finish it off easily. The great white's diet changes as it grows older. Young sharks of about 7–10 ft (2–3 m) long eat mostly fish; older sharks around 13 ft (4 m) long tackle larger prey such as seals and sea lions.

ON THE MENU
Great whites eat a variety of animals including bony fish, other sharks, some seabirds, marine mammals (such as seals and porpoises), and, occasionally, people! Great whites are also scavengers and will eat whale carcasses and other dead animals. Unless a great white is seen feeding, it is hard to know if an animal found in its stomach had already died before it was eaten.

Diver for dinner

Leopard sharks (above) are eaten by young great whites along the Pacific coast of North America

Bony fish, such as cabezon (above), are eaten by young great whites along the Pacific coast of North America

California sea lions (right) are eaten by adult great whites

Scientists have found remains of jackass penguins, from South Africa, with bite marks made by great whites

TOP TIGER
Tigers and great whites are the top predators of land and sea, respectively. When they're adults, no animals prey on them, but they are killed by people. Tigers, like great whites, sometimes eat people.

Young elephant seals (above) are easy prey

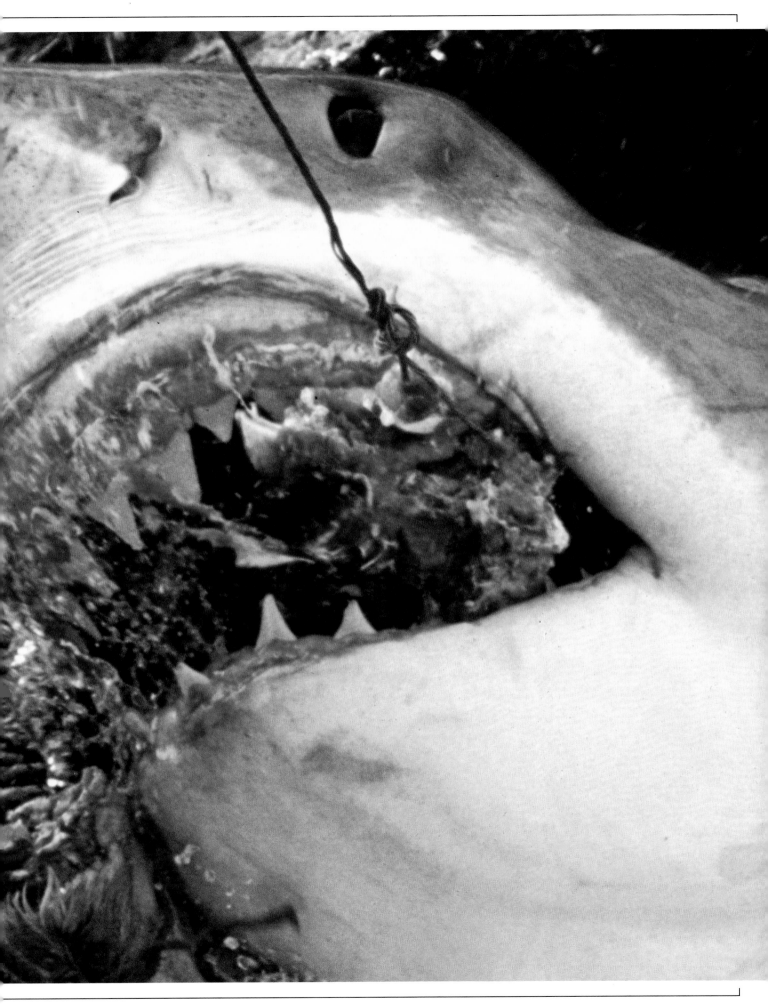

Gentle giants

HUMPBACK WHALES
Whale sharks are named after those other ocean giants – the whales – which are not fish but mammals.

Whale sharks are the largest fish in the world, reaching at least 40 ft (12 m) long and weighing 13 tons (13.2 tonnes), about as large as an adult gray whale. These docile sharks are harmless and will allow scuba divers to hitch rides by hanging onto their fins; the only danger is in getting scraped by the shark's rough skin, or accidentally knocked by the huge tail as it swings back and forth. These giant fish cruise at 2 mph (3 kph). They live in tropical and subtropical waters, and they feed by filtering food out of the water. Because they feed near the surface, where there is a good supply of food to support their large bulk, they occasionally run into ships. Scientists believe that whale sharks may either lay enormous 14-in (30-cm) long eggs or give birth to live young, hatched from eggs inside their bodies.

Distribution of whale sharks

AT THE DENTIST
People use their teeth to chew food. If their teeth are removed, they need to replace them with false ones.

NOT MUCH OF A BITE
Whale sharks do not bite or chew food, so they do not need their teeth, which are no bigger than a match head.

A GREAT GULP
Despite their huge size, whale sharks feed on plankton (tiny animals that drift in the sea), small fish, and squid. Other large fish, such as basking sharks (pp. 34–35), manta rays (pp. 8–9), and baleen whales, also feed by filtering food out of the water. Whale sharks scoop up water into their huge mouths, and as water passes over their gills and out through their gill slits, food is captured in filters attached to the gills. These filters are made up of a mesh of tissues supported by cartilaginous rods. Whale sharks occasionally eat larger fish such as mackerel and tuna, which are swallowed as they scoop up schools of smaller fish. They can feed in a vertical position, even sticking their heads out of the water and sinking down to draw large fish into their mouths.

White-spotted
bamboo sharks
grow to about
37 in (95 cm) long

Anal fin

Brown-banded bamboo
sharks grow to just
over 3.3 ft (1 m)
long

Nurse sharks grow
to 10 ft (3 m)
long

Barbel

Epaulette sharks grow to just over 3.3 ft (1 m)
long

ONE BIG HAPPY FAMILY
Although they are much smaller, these four
sharks (white-spotted and brown-banded
bamboos, nurse, and epaulette) all belong
to the same group as the whale shark. The
main features they have in common are the
presence of an anal fin and the position of
their mouths well in front of their eyes.
They also have two barbels on the tips of
their snouts that help them find food.
Unlike the whale shark, these much
smaller sharks all live on the seabed.

Basking beauties

With their huge mouths wide open, basking sharks cruise the ocean like giant mobile sieves, filtering countless tiny creatures from the water. This shark is the second largest fish in the world, after the whale shark (pp. 32–33); it grows to about 33 ft (10 m) long and weighs over 3.6 tons (4 tonnes). Basking sharks often swim at the surface on sunny days with their dorsal fins, and perhaps their snouts or tails out of the water. They are probably more attracted by the concentration of food at the surface than by the sunshine. Unfortunately, when the sharks are at the surface, they make easy targets for fishermen who harpoon them for the oil in their large livers, which may be a quarter of their body weight. These sharks are also killed because of the damage they do to salmon nets. Naturalists are concerned that too many are being killed; little is yet known about these fish – how they reproduce, how they migrate, and how many are left in the wild.

SHARK FISHING
At Achill Island off Ireland's northwest coast, basking sharks were once netted in a bay, then speared with a lance, and dragged ashore. Fishing stopped when the numbers of sharks coming into the bay declined.

Eye

Nostril

Gill arch – water passes through the arch and then through a sieve of gill rakers before flowing over the gills and out through the gill slits

OILY MOUTHS
Oil from sharks' livers has been used in cosmetics like lipsticks.

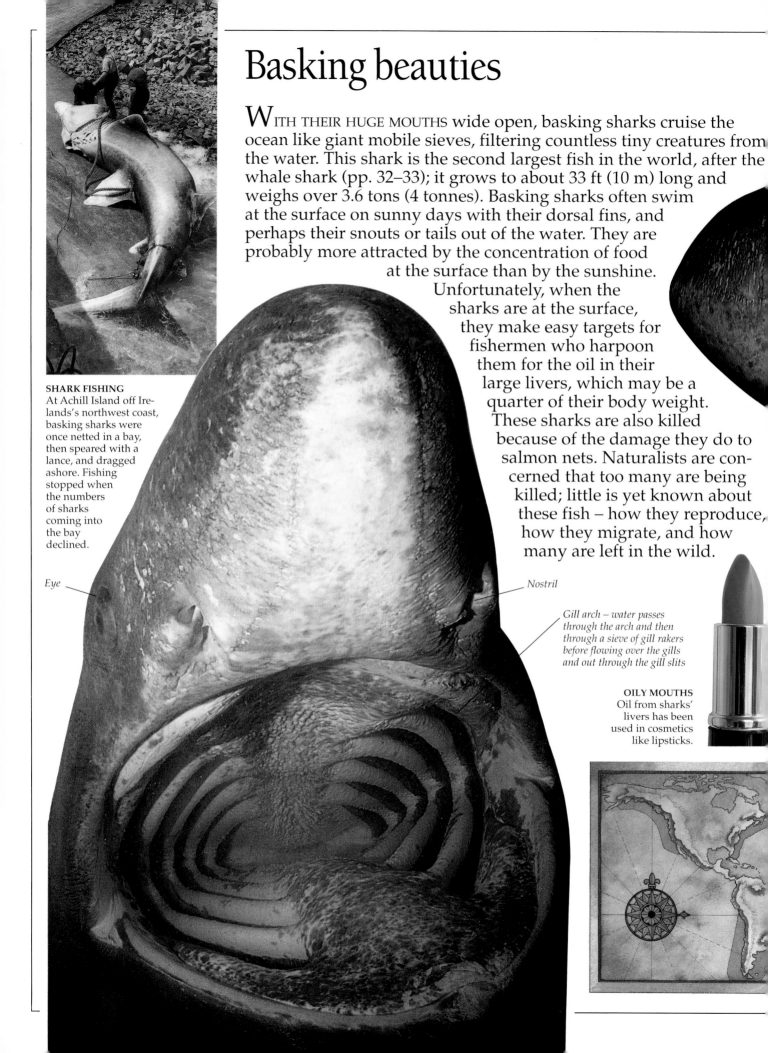

Nostril

Eye

Gill rakers

Open mouth of basking shark

Distribution of basking sharks

0   1200   2400   3600 mi

OPENMOUTHED

As the basking shark swims along, 400,000 gallons (1.5 million liters) of water flow through its huge mouth each hour. Drifting in the water are tiny creatures like baby crabs, fish eggs, copepods, and arrowworms – all known as plankton – which are strained out of the water by hundreds of long bristles, or gill rakers (pp. 24–25), and trapped in a layer of slime. After a minute the basking shark closes its mouth, emptying the water out through its gill slits before swallowing its food. In winter, when plankton becomes scarce in the cool waters where basking sharks live, they stop feeding and shed their gill rakers. No one knows where basking sharks go in winter, but they may sink to the bottom to rest on the seabed. In spring, basking sharks appear on the water's surface and start to feed again, having grown a new set of gill rakers.

SHARKS AT WAR

In World War II some fighter planes used shark oil to lubri-cate their instruments. These American planes are decorated with shark jaws to frighten the enemy, but the painted sharks have much bigger teeth than basking sharks do.

Angel sharks

IMAGINE RUNNING A STEAMROLLER over a normal-shaped shark – the result would look very much like an angel shark. These strange, flat sharks have extra-large pectoral fins, which resemble angels' wings. Angel sharks spend much of their lives resting on the seabed or lying in wait for fish or shellfish to move within reach of their snapping, sharp-toothed jaws. They can also swim, using their tails to propel themselves along, just as other kinds of shark do. Angel sharks are most active between dusk and dawn, traveling as far as 5.5 miles (9 km) during the night. There are 13 species of angel shark that live in shallow coastal waters around the world and to depths of over 3,300 ft (1,000 km).

MONK FISH
Ever since the 16th century, angel sharks have been called "monk fish," because the shape of their head looks like the hood on a monk's cloak.

The caudal fin, or lower lobe of the tail, is longer than the upper lobe – a feature unique to angel sharks

Second dorsal fin

| 0 | 1200 | 2400 | 3600 | miles |

Distribution of angel sharks

Pelvic fin

First dorsal fin

Gill slit

Mouth

Eye

Spiracle

Pelvic fin

LOOKALIKES
Rays (pp. 8–9) are flat, just like angel sharks. But unlike angel sharks' pectoral fins, a ray's are completely attached to its head, and its gill slits are located on the underside of its body.

Underside of ray

Pectoral fin

Top side of ray

ANGELS
This angel shark grows to nearly 6.5 ft (2 m) long. It is found in the Mediterranean and Baltic seas, the eastern Atlantic Ocean, and the English Channel, down to depths of about 490 ft (150 m). Like all angel sharks, it has eyes on the top of its head so it can see while lying flat on the seabed. For respiration (breathing), it draws in water through its large spiracles, which are also on the top of its head. Water taken in through the spiracles is more likely to be free of silt, which could clog up its gills, than water taken in through its mouth.

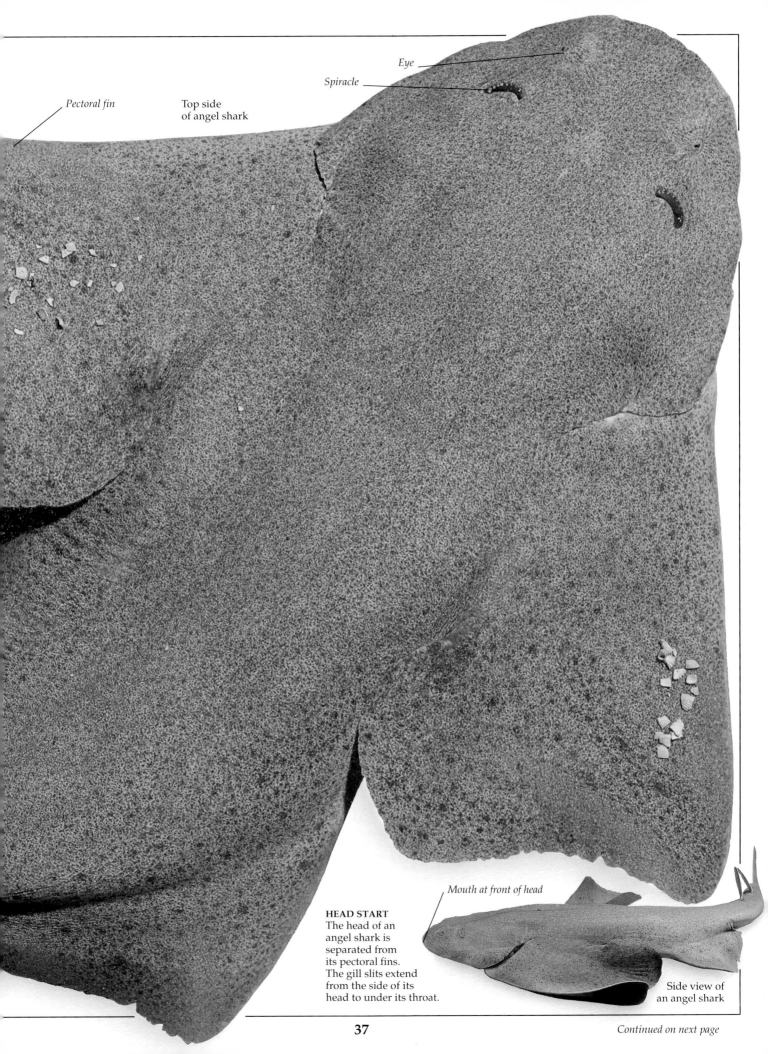

Pectoral fin

Top side
of angel shark

Eye

Spiracle

HEAD START
The head of an
angel shark is
separated from
its pectoral fins.
The gill slits extend
from the side of its
head to under its throat.

Mouth at front of head

Side view of
an angel shark

37

Continued on next page

Japanese wobbegong

Lobe

Barbel

SECRET AGENT
Spies work undercover
on secret missions.
Some kinds of shark
are secretive too, and
hide from predators by
using camouflage.

**WOBBEGONG
OF THE ORIENT**
The Japanese
wobbegong lives along the
coasts of Japan, China,
Vietnam, the Philippines,
and Korea, in the western
Pacific. It grows to about
3.3 ft (1 m) in length.
Wobbegongs are not
usually aggressive,
but people have
been bitten when they have stepped
on a hidden wobbegong by mistake.
Fishermen have also been bitten by
wobbegongs caught in their nets.

FANTÔMAS
L'AGENT SECRET

Undercover sharks

Sharks living on the seabed often have
colors and patterns on their skin. These
sharks, such as wobbegongs and swell
and angel sharks, are able to camouflage themselves, or to blend in with
their surroundings. They have
blotches, spots, or stripes that
make them difficult to see on
sand or among rocks, sea-
weeds, and corals on the seabed.
Wobbegongs have elaborate
disguises, with blotchy skin and
lobes on their head that look like bits of
seaweed. Other sharks, like swell
sharks, hide in crevices; angel sharks
cover themselves with sand. Why hide
if you are a shark with sharp teeth?
These undercover sharks often lie in
wait for prey like fish and crabs to
swim near, then snap them up. Also,
hiding helps small sharks avoid
being eaten by larger predators.

**NOW YOU SEE ME,
NOW YOU DON'T**
It is difficult to see
angel sharks lying o
the seabed – the
are flat and their
mottled skin loo
like sand (top left). To
complete their super
disguise, angel shark
(pp. 36–37) partially
bury themselves in th
sand by shuffling the
pectoral fins and
flicking the sand ove
their backs (center
left). When the shark
under a layer of sand
its eyes poke above t
surface (bottom left)
keeping a look out fo
prey. When a fish
comes near, the ange
shark lunges
forward, snapping
its jaws shut
around it. If diver
approach, they may
leave their hiding
place and swim off.
Fishermen catch ang
sharks in nets towed
across the seabed.

AUSTRALIAN SHARK WITH A BEARD
The tasseled wobbegong's beard has
many branched lobes around its
mouth. Its prey – fish and shrimp –
may mistake these for seaweed
and end up being eaten.

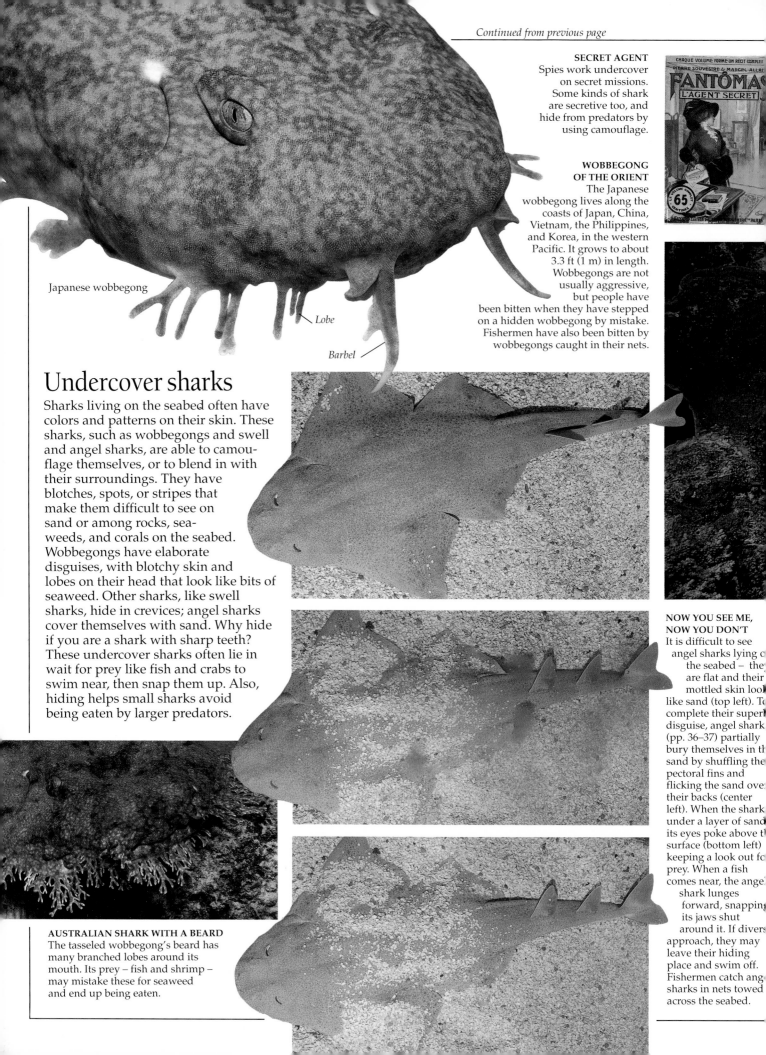

MUG SHOTS
Like a prisoner's mug shots, this ornate wobbegong looks different from different angles – from above (top left) and from the side (bottom left). The wobbegong's disguise works just as well from any direction. The Aborigines of Australia gave wobbegongs their wonderful name.

If attacked, a swell shark hides in a crevice and gulps down water, swelling up so that it jams itself in and cannot be pried out.

WHERE'S THE TASSELED WOBBEGONG?
Out of all six wobbegong species, this one has the most branched lobes, or tassels, on its head. Its beard extends around the mouth and down its chin.

Ornate wobbegong

Barbel

LIFE ON THE SEABED
Wobbegongs spend much of the day lurking on the seabed in the shallows and even in rock pools. They are flat, and their eyes and spiracles are on the upper side of their head, like angel sharks. All wobbegongs have an anal fin; angel sharks lack them. The lobes around their mouth are outgrowths of skin. Even the wobbegong's barbels, or whiskers, on its rounded snout look like fronds of seaweed.

Lobe

Horn sharks

HORN SHARKS ARE NAMED FOR the two spines on their backs next to each dorsal fin, which look like small horns. The sharks in this group are also called bull-heads because they have broad heads with ridges above their eyes. The shape of the head and the presence of an anal fin distinguish horn sharks from spiny dogfish, which also have dorsal spines.

Practicing the horn makes perfect

There are eight species of horn shark; most are no longer than 5 ft (1.5 m). They are found in the Pacific and Indian oceans, where they live on the seabed in shallow water. Horn sharks swim with slow beats of their tails and push themselves along the bottom with their pectoral fins. The Australian Port Jackson sharks can travel long distances, covering over 500 miles (800 km) to visit their breeding sites. Because horn sharks are slow, scuba divers sometimes tease them by pulling their tails. But they've been known to bite back. Sadly, horn sharks are killed for their spines, which are used to make jewelry (pp. 60–61).

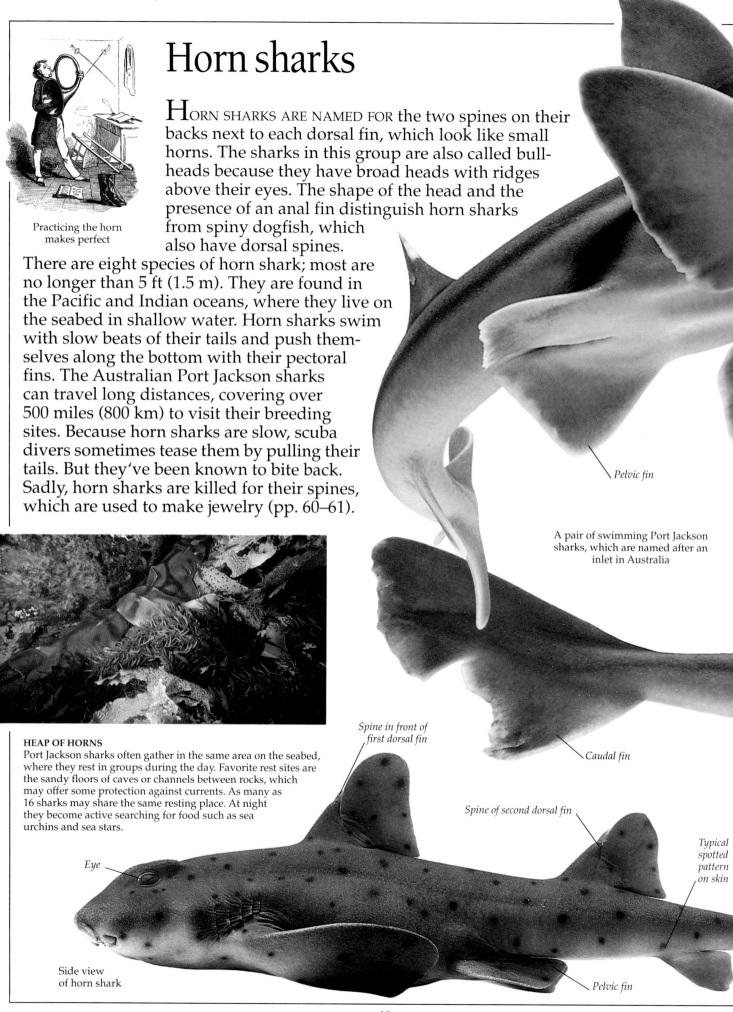

Pelvic fin

A pair of swimming Port Jackson sharks, which are named after an inlet in Australia

HEAP OF HORNS
Port Jackson sharks often gather in the same area on the seabed, where they rest in groups during the day. Favorite rest sites are the sandy floors of caves or channels between rocks, which may offer some protection against currents. As many as 16 sharks may share the same resting place. At night they become active searching for food such as sea urchins and sea stars.

Spine in front of first dorsal fin

Caudal fin

Spine of second dorsal fin

Typical spotted pattern on skin

Eye

Side view of horn shark

Pelvic fin

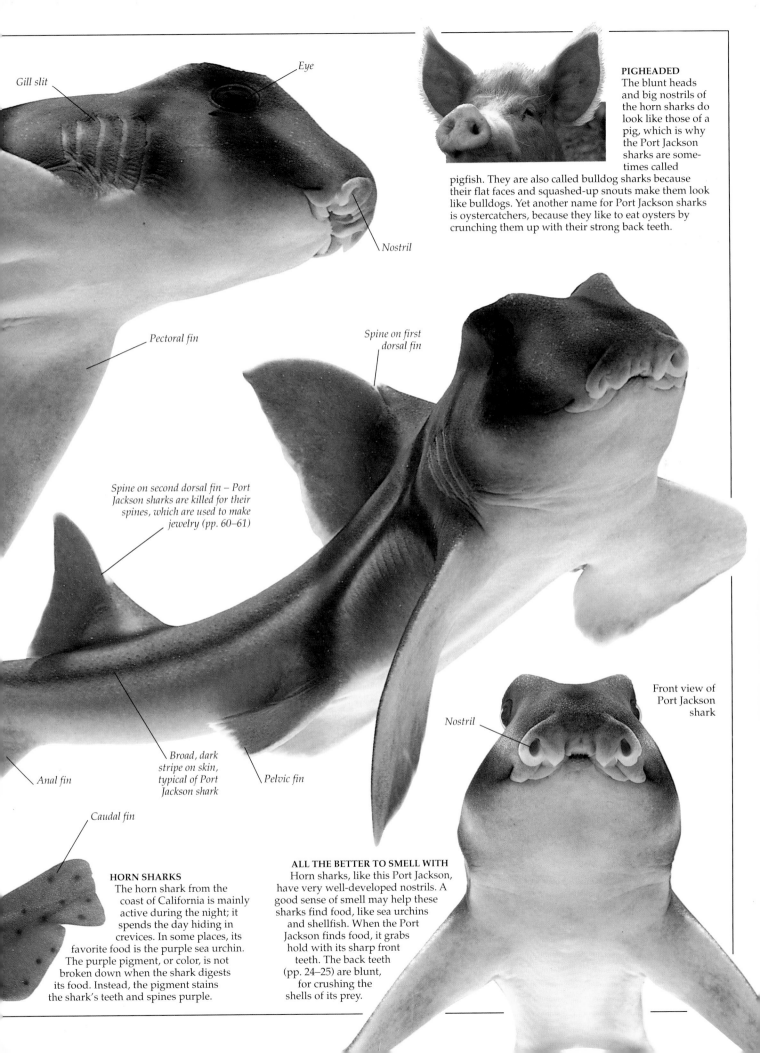

Gill slit

Eye

Nostril

PIGHEADED
The blunt heads and big nostrils of the horn sharks do look like those of a pig, which is why the Port Jackson sharks are sometimes called pigfish. They are also called bulldog sharks because their flat faces and squashed-up snouts make them look like bulldogs. Yet another name for Port Jackson sharks is oystercatchers, because they like to eat oysters by crunching them up with their strong back teeth.

Pectoral fin

Spine on first dorsal fin

Spine on second dorsal fin – Port Jackson sharks are killed for their spines, which are used to make jewelry (pp. 60–61)

Nostril

Front view of Port Jackson shark

Anal fin

Broad, dark stripe on skin, typical of Port Jackson shark

Pelvic fin

Caudal fin

HORN SHARKS
The horn shark from the coast of California is mainly active during the night; it spends the day hiding in crevices. In some places, its favorite food is the purple sea urchin. The purple pigment, or color, is not broken down when the shark digests its food. Instead, the pigment stains the shark's teeth and spines purple.

ALL THE BETTER TO SMELL WITH
Horn sharks, like this Port Jackson, have very well-developed nostrils. A good sense of smell may help these sharks find food, like sea urchins and shellfish. When the Port Jackson finds food, it grabs hold with its sharp front teeth. The back teeth (pp. 24–25) are blunt, for crushing the shells of its prey.

Head like a hammer

OF ALL THE SHARKS, hammerheads have the strangest-shaped heads. There are nine species of hammerhead, including the bonnetheads, which have only small head projections. The winghead shark has by far the widest head; its head can be half as long as its body. Most hammerheads live in warm temperate and tropical coastal waters. The scalloped hammerhead is one of the most common species and is found in warm waters throughout the world. Large schools of scalloped hammerheads often congregate in areas where there are features on the sea floor like undersea peaks, or sea mounts. A hundred of these sharks may form a school, all of them swimming in unison. At dusk they swim off on their own to feed, and then at dawn they regroup in the same place.

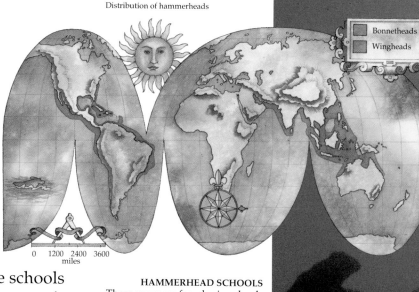

Distribution of hammerheads

Bonnetheads
Wingheads

0   1200   2400   3600
miles

HAMMERHEAD SCHOOLS
There are more females in schools than males, but the reason why they group together is unclear. These large predators have few enemies, so it's not likely that they school for protection. The females compete with each other (often butting one another) to stay in the center of the schools. This may give them a better chance to be courted by the males.

DIFFICULT DIET
Stingrays are the favorite food of the great hammerhead even though the rays are armed with one or more venomous spines, or "stingers," on their tails. Hammerheads do not seem to mind being stung – one individual had nearly a hundred spines sticking into its mouth and gullet.

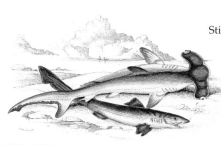

TWO DIFFERENT SHARKS
The shape of the hammerhead's head (top) compared to that of other sharks – like the tope (bottom) – fascinated early naturalists.

A FINE BONNET
Bonnetheads are the smallest of the hammerheads, reaching only 5 ft (1.5 m) long. The great hammerhead can grow as long as 19.5 ft (6 m). They usually swim together in small groups, but sometimes huge schools of hundreds of sharks congregate near the surface.

Mouth

Gill slit

First dorsal fin

Pectoral fin

WHY A HAMMER?
No one knows why a hammerhead has a hammer-shaped head, but the broad, flat head may give extra lift to the front of the shark's body as it swims. These two hammerheads (right) differ slightly in that the scalloped one (left) has an indentation in the middle of its head, while the smooth, or common, one does not.

Bonnethead shark

Anal fin   *Pelvic fin*

HEAD ON
Hammerheads swing their heads from side to side as they swim along, which gives them an exellent all-around view, since their eyes are right at the tips of their hammers. Their broad heads bear many ampullae of Lorenzini, which sense tiny electric currents generated by their prey.

Scalloped
hammerhead

Weird and wonderful

ONE OF THE WORLD'S most extraordinary sharks, the megamouth, was only discovered in 1976. No one had come across this large shark before, though it is over 16 ft (5 m) long and weighs 1,500 lb (680 kg). Since 1976 five more megamouths have been found, including one that was captured alive off the coast of California in 1990. Scientists attached radio tags to this living megamouth so they could follow it (pp. 54–55). The shark spent the day at 450–500 ft (135-150 m) down, feeding on krill (shrimplike creatures). After sunset it ascended to within 40 ft (12 m) of the surface, following its food source, before its descent into the depths at dawn. Another strange shark, the goblin shark, was found nearly 100 years ago, yet scientists know little about it. Other mysteries have been solved. No one knew what caused disk-shaped bites on seals, whales, and dolphins, but the culprits were found to be cookiecutter sharks. Who knows what other weird and wonderful sharks are still to be found deep in the ocean?

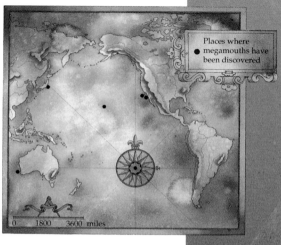

Places where megamouths have been discovered

BIG MOUTH
Megamouth means "big mouth," a good name for a shark with a 3-ft (1-m) grin. This shark may lure krill into its huge mouth with luminous organs around its lips. The first megamouth was brought up dead from 660 ft (200 m), entangled in the sea anchor of a U.S. Navy boat off Hawaii. The second was caught in gill nets (long nets in which fish are trapped) off California; the third was washed up and died on a beach near Perth, Australia; a fourth was found dead and a fifth alive off the coast of Japan. The sixth was caught and released off the California coast.

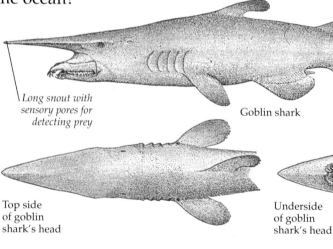

Long snout with sensory pores for detecting prey

Goblin shark

Top side of goblin shark's head

Underside of goblin shark's head

REALLY WEIRD
These ugly sharks (above) were first discovered by scientists off the coast of Japan in 1898. They have flabby bodies and are over 10 ft (3 m) long. Not much is known about these rare sharks that live in deep water at least 530 ft (160 m) down.

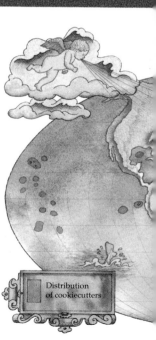

Distribution of cookiecutters

GLOWS IN THE DARK
This is one of the lantern sharks, which live in the oceans' dark depths. They are called lantern sharks because they are luminous, or glow in the dark. They are probably the world's smallest sharks, growing to only 8 in (20 cm) long.

BITE SIZED
Cookiecutters have large teeth for sharks only 1.7 ft (0.5 m) long. The common cookiecutter (one of two species) uses its teeth to cut out chunks of flesh from large fish as well as whales, seals, and dolphins. It may wait for such large animals to approach it rather than chasing after them. The cookie-cutter forms a suction cup with its lips, bites, then swivels around to take an oval-shaped plug of flesh. Cookiecutters have also taken bites out of the rubber components of submarines and undersea cables.

GODDESS OF LIGHT
The cookiecutters' scientific genus name, *Isistius*, is from Isis, the Egyptian goddess of light. Cookie-cutters have many light organs on their bellies and glow in the dark. This may attract prey like whales to come close enough to be bitten.

BORING BITES
The wounds on this seal were made by a cookiecutter shark biting into its flesh.

200   2400   3600 miles

Shark artifacts

FOR CENTURIES, people around the world have caught sharks and taken their teeth and skin to make a wide variety of objects, or artifacts. Shark teeth are so sharp that early people were able to make tools and weapons from them. Sharkskin is so hard-wearing that it could be used to make shoes, as well as grips or sheaths for swords and daggers (pp. 60–61). Early people who caught sharks had great respect for these magnificent predators. Fishing for sharks with primitive tools was difficult and dangerous, and stories and legends about sharks were common among seafaring and island people. Sharks were even regarded as gods and were worshipped on some islands in the Pacific. In comparison, early Europeans have few myths about sharks, but sharks do appear in their early natural history books (pp. 28–29).

MONKEY BUSINESS
This monkey head was made of precious stones by the Aztecs in Mexico. Its teeth are those of a shark.

Large, serrated tooth, probably from a great white shark (pp. 28–31)

CROWN JEWEL
The ten shark teeth that went into making this decorative necklace probably came from great white sharks caught off the coast of New Zealand, where the native Maori live. Today's shark-tooth jewelry, made specially for tourists, contributes to the abuse, rather than the use, of sharks (pp. 60–61).

Pair of fisherman's shoes, made of sharkskin, from India

Sharkskin

Shark-shaped gold weight from Ghana in West Africa

Tin toy, in the form of a shark, from Malaysia

Shark tooth

Shark tooth

Tool, tipped with a shark's tooth, for tattooing people's skin, from Kiribati (the Gilbert Islands), in the western Pacific Ocean

Carved wooden drum, with sharkskin-covered top, 18th century, from the Hawaiian islands in the Pacific

Wooden rasp, covered in sharkskin, from the island of Santa Cruz in the south-west Pacific (below)

Shark skin

Sharkskin-covered grater (below) from the Wallis Islands in the Pacific

Wood knife (right), with cutting edge made of sharks' teeth, from Greenland

Shark skin

SHARKS IN THE HOME
From ancient times, the skin and teeth of sharks have been used to make a variety of household items. Some sharkskin is so rough that it has been used for grating food (left), but if the denticles are removed the soft skin is used like leather for making shoes and belts, or even drums (above). Shark teeth have been used for knives, jewelry, and tools. Other items were made in the shape of a shark because people admired sharks, but toy sharks were made just for fun, as they are today.

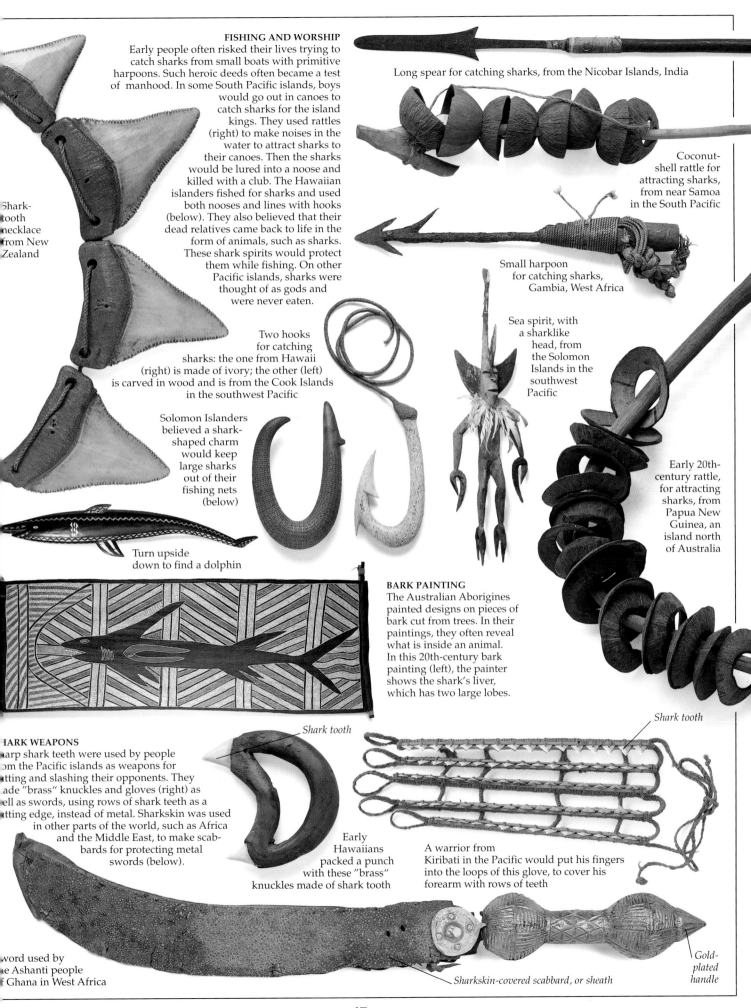

FISHING AND WORSHIP

Early people often risked their lives trying to catch sharks from small boats with primitive harpoons. Such heroic deeds often became a test of manhood. In some South Pacific islands, boys would go out in canoes to catch sharks for the island kings. They used rattles (right) to make noises in the water to attract sharks to their canoes. Then the sharks would be lured into a noose and killed with a club. The Hawaiian islanders fished for sharks and used both nooses and lines with hooks (below). They also believed that their dead relatives came back to life in the form of animals, such as sharks. These shark spirits would protect them while fishing. On other Pacific islands, sharks were thought of as gods and were never eaten.

Long spear for catching sharks, from the Nicobar Islands, India

Coconut-shell rattle for attracting sharks, from near Samoa in the South Pacific

Small harpoon for catching sharks, Gambia, West Africa

Shark-tooth necklace from New Zealand

Sea spirit, with a sharklike head, from the Solomon Islands in the southwest Pacific

Two hooks for catching sharks: the one from Hawaii (right) is made of ivory; the other (left) is carved in wood and is from the Cook Islands in the southwest Pacific

Solomon Islanders believed a shark-shaped charm would keep large sharks out of their fishing nets (below)

Turn upside down to find a dolphin

Early 20th-century rattle, for attracting sharks, from Papua New Guinea, an island north of Australia

BARK PAINTING

The Australian Aborigines painted designs on pieces of bark cut from trees. In their paintings, they often reveal what is inside an animal. In this 20th-century bark painting (left), the painter shows the shark's liver, which has two large lobes.

Shark tooth

SHARK WEAPONS

Sharp shark teeth were used by people from the Pacific islands as weapons for cutting and slashing their opponents. They made "brass" knuckles and gloves (right) as well as swords, using rows of shark teeth as a cutting edge, instead of metal. Sharkskin was used in other parts of the world, such as Africa and the Middle East, to make scabbards for protecting metal swords (below).

Shark tooth

Early Hawaiians packed a punch with these "brass" knuckles made of shark tooth

A warrior from Kiribati in the Pacific would put his fingers into the loops of this glove, to cover his forearm with rows of teeth

Sword used by the Ashanti people of Ghana in West Africa

Gold-plated handle

Sharkskin-covered scabbard, or sheath

Shark attack

ATTACK AT SEA
Prisoners escaping from Devil's Island off Guyana are attacked by sharks.

Mᴏsᴛ sʜᴀʀᴋs are not dangerous and will leave people alone. Each year 50 to 75 people are reported attacked by sharks, but only 5 to 10 of these attacks result in death. People are more likely to die in car accidents or drown in the ocean than be killed by a shark. Attacks may occur when a shark mistakes a person for usual prey – a person's foot may look like a fish. A shark may attack if it feels threatened or is provoked. It is dangerous to be in water where there may be sharks, if for example, the water is murky, you have cut yourself, or bait has been put out for fish. Pay attention to local authorities – never swim alone or at night.

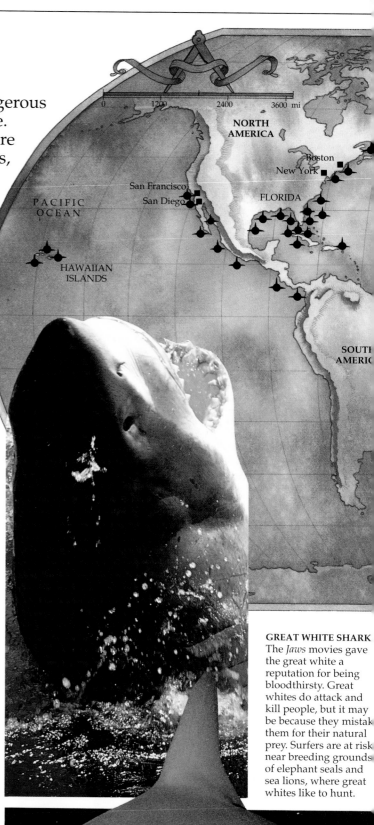

WOUNDED SEAL
Elephant seals are what most great whites on the California coast feast on. These sharks usually approach their prey from behind and then take a bite out of it. They wait until the victim is weakened from loss of blood before finishing it off. Sometimes the seal manages to escape by reaching the beach before the shark attacks again.

FATAL SHARK ATTACK
Most fatal shark attacks occur where people surf, swim, or scuba dive, and where there are large sharks, like the great white, swimming close to shore. Attacks can also occur on people escaping from sinking ships or plane crashes far out at sea. Each year the International Shark Attack File records the numbers of attacks reported.

Each year an average of 92 people die by drowning in the sea off Australia's coast . . .

. . . while around eight people die from scuba diving accidents . . .

. . . and less than one person dies from a shark attack.

WARNING SIGN
To avoid being attacked by sharks, pay attention to signs like this one. Sharks may attack people wading in shallow water.

BULL SHARK
The bull shark is one of the four most dangerous sharks in the world, along with the great white, oceanic whitetip, and tiger sharks. The bull shark lives in the warm oceans of the world. It is one of the few sharks that spends time in fresh water, swimming far up rivers such as South America's Amazon and Africa's Zambezi. It can also enter lakes. At 10 ft (3 m) long, bull sharks are large enough to tackle a person and are not fussy what they eat.

GREAT WHITE SHARK
The *Jaws* movies gave the great white a reputation for being bloodthirsty. Great whites do attack and kill people, but it may be because they mistake them for their natural prey. Surfers are at risk near breeding grounds of elephant seals and sea lions, where great whites like to hunt.

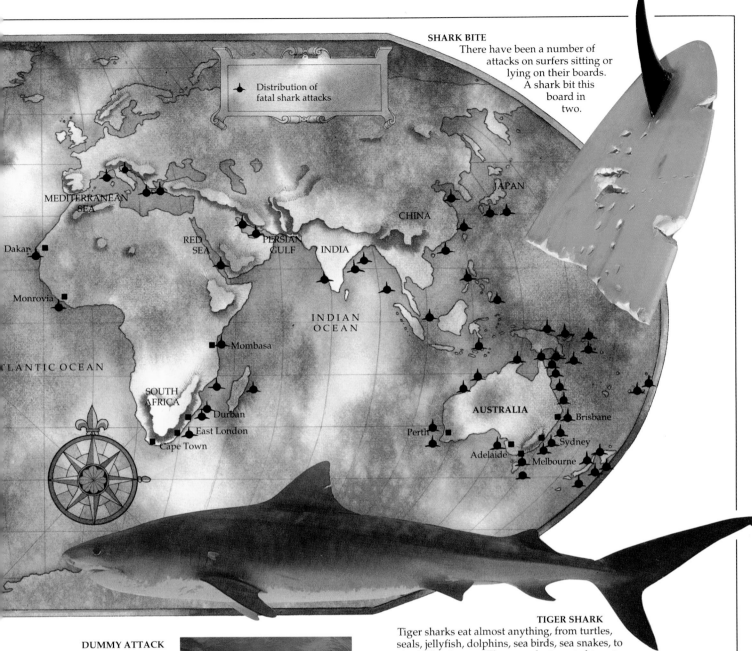

SHARK BITE
There have been a number of attacks on surfers sitting or lying on their boards. A shark bit this board in two.

Distribution of fatal shark attacks

MEDITERRANEAN SEA

Dakar

Monrovia

ATLANTIC OCEAN

RED SEA

PERSIAN GULF

INDIA

INDIAN OCEAN

CHINA

JAPAN

Mombasa

SOUTH AFRICA

Durban

East London

Cape Town

AUSTRALIA

Perth

Adelaide

Melbourne

Brisbane

Sydney

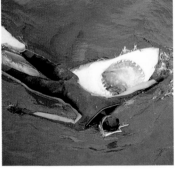

DUMMY ATTACK
Wet suits do not protect against shark attack, as this experiment with a dummy shows, nor do colored or patterned wet suits repel sharks.

SHARK'S-EYE VIEW
Attacks on surfers occur near seal or sea lion breeding colonies, when surfers have dangled their arms or legs over the edge of their surf boards. Sharks can mistake surfers for seals because they have similar shapes when seen from below.

TIGER SHARK
Tiger sharks eat almost anything, from turtles, seals, jellyfish, dolphins, sea birds, sea snakes, to junk like tin cans. They may be tempted to eat any animal, including people.

NORMAL SWIMMING
Gray reef sharks live near coral reefs in the Indian and Pacific oceans and grow to about 8 ft (2.5 m) long. During normal swimming, the back is gently curved and the pectoral fins held straight out from the body.

THREAT POSTURE
If a diver approaches too close or surprises a gray reef shark, it may adopt this threat posture. The shark arches its back and holds its pectoral fins downward. It may also swim around in a figure eight. If the diver does not swim slowly away, the shark may attack.

Sharks at bay

PEOPLE WHO GO into the water where there may be dangerous sharks run a small risk of being attacked. There is no simple way to keep sharks away from all the places where people wade, swim, surf, or scuba dive. Shark-proof enclosures have been built, but these can only protect small areas because of the large cost. In South Africa and Australia, nets are used along the most popular beaches to trap sharks. These nets also trap and kill many harmless sharks, dolphins, rays, and turtles. Tests are being done to see if electric barriers can be used that would keep sharks away without killing them or other animals. Scuba divers occasionally carry bangsticks (tipped with an explosive cartridge), but often an inquisitive shark can be simply pushed away with a long, sturdy stick or club. If all else fails, kicking or punching a shark's snout may discourage them from attacking.

JONAH AND THE ?
In the Bible story, Jonah was swallowed by a large sea creature, which could have been a shark, instead of a whale, as the story claims.

LIFEGUARDS
Australian lifeguards must watch ou[t] for sharks. If sharks are spotted near [the] beach, the shark alarm is sounded an[d] swimmers leave the water. The beach may be closed for the rest of the day, [if] sharks stay in the area. Always follow [the] lifeguard's advice on safe swimming.

BLOWN AWAY!
A tiger shark is brought aboard after being killed with a bangstick. The stick fires on contact, tearing apart the shark's insides.

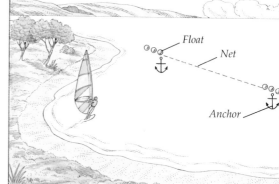

Float
Net
Anchor

IN THE BAG
One way to help people who end up in the sea if a ship sinks or an airplane crashes is to give them large inflatable bags. When the U.S. Navy tested the bags, sharks avoided them, because they could not see any limbs, sense any electric signals, or smell blood or body wastes, which are kept in the bag.

ONE LESS SHARK
A shark, trapped in a mesh net off an Australian beach (right), is landed. During a 17-month period in the 1930s, 1,500 sharks were caught by this method. Since then numbers of sharks have decreased sharply.

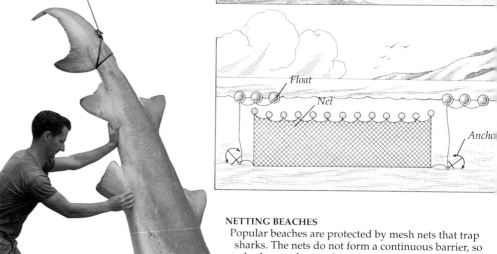

Float
Net
Ancho[r]

NETTING BEACHES
Popular beaches are protected by mesh nets that trap sharks. The nets do not form a continuous barrier, so sharks may be caught swimming either toward or away from the beach. Heavy anchors keep the nets on or close to the bottom, and floats keep the top of the net suspended in the water. The nets are about 330 ft (100 m) long and 20 ft (6 m) deep. Marker buoys float at the surface so the nets are easily found again. The nets are checked almost every day and dead sea animals removed. After three weeks the nets need to be replaced because they become fouled by seaweed and other marine growth, and so can easily be seen and avoided by sharks. Nets that have become tangled up in storm waves also need to be replaced.

CHAIN WALL

This wall (left) of interlinked chains surrounding an Australian beach prevents any sharks from getting in. Such walls are too costly to protect more than a couple of miles of beach. Chemical repellents have also been tried, but they are not effective, as any substance released around a person in the water disperses too quickly in the waves.

INVISIBLE BARRIER

Sharks are very sensitive to electric currents, and here an invisible electric barrier is being tested. When the current is off (top) the lemon shark swims past, but when the current is switched on (left) the shark turns back to avoid it. Cables and even portable devices that produce electrical pulses to deter sharks have been tested in the sea.

PROTECTED BEACH

Experiments using screens made of bubbles released from air hoses on the seabed have been tried, but shark nets, as on this Australian beach (above), still seem to offer the best protection.

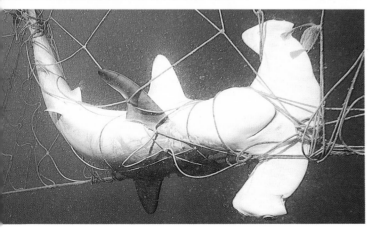

DEATH NETS

Mesh nets, used to protect beaches, kill many sharks, like the great white (above) and hammerhead (left). Trapped sharks suffocate: when a shark can't swim, it can't keep water flowing over its gills. Up to 1,400 sharks – many of which are harmless – plus many dolphins, are caught each year in South African nets.

SHARK REPELLENT

The American scientist Dr. Eugenie Clark discovered that the Moses sole from the Red Sea produces its own shark repellent. When the sole is attacked, milky, toxic secretions ooze out its skin, so the shark spits it out.

51

In the cage and out

DIVING SUIT
In the early 19th century, divers wore heavy helmets or hard hats and had air pumped down tubes from the surface. Tall tales were often told about attacks by giant octopuses.

DIVING WITH LARGE predatory sharks can be dangerous, so people who want to get close to sharks, like underwater photographers and film-makers, use a strong metal cage to protect themselves. No one sensible would want to be in the water with a great white shark (pp. 28–31), unless protected by a cage. For smaller and less dangerous species, like blue sharks (pp. 56–57), divers sometimes wear chain-mail suits. The chain mail is sufficiently strong to keep the shark's teeth from penetrating the skin if it should bite, but bruising can still occur. Divers may also have a cage just to retreat into, should the sharks become aggressive. Chum (pp. 28–29) and baits are put in the water to attract sharks, which may become excited by the presence of food and snap at the divers. When sharks are being filmed or photographed from outside a cage, safety divers should also be present to keep watch for sharks approaching from outside the filmmaker's field of vision.

1 LOWERING THE CAGE INTO WATER
Once the dive boat reaches the right place for great whites, chum is thrown into the water, creating an oily slick, and the metal cage is lowered into the sea.

2 A GREAT WHITE APPROACHES
It may be several days before a great white comes close to the cage, kept on the water's sur-face by floats. The diver can close the lid of the cage for complete protection, if a shark closes in.

3 A VIEW FROM INSIDE THE CAGE
Baits such as horsemeat and tuna attract the shark near the cage. The bars are close enough together to p vent the great white from biting the photographer, bu sharks, attracted by metal, may bite the boat and cage

IN SHINING ARMOR
Famous shark film-maker Valerie Taylor tests the effectiveness of the chain-mail suit. The blue shark (left) is tempted to bite because the sleeve of the suit has been stuffed with pieces of fish. Problems may occur if the shark gets its teeth caught in the chain mail – in its struggle to get free, it could pull Valerie's glove right off. The suits are also heavy, so swimming is difficult. Chain mail was first used by medieval knights to protect themselves from being slashed by swords. Nowadays, butchers also use chain-mail gloves (top) to protect their hands from being cut when they slice meat.

FILMING SHARKS
Australian film-makers Ron and Valerie Taylor are well known for their work on sharks. Ron Taylor films a white-tip reef shark taking a bait (right), while a blue shark approaches the camera (below right).

GREAT WHITE SWIMS BY
Divers can be shaken off their feet if a werful great white should bump into their ze. Such close-up views of the sharks reveal t how big these awesome creatures really are.

Studying sharks

It is difficult to study sharks in the wild, because they constantly move around, swim too fast, and dive too deep for divers to keep up with them. Some sharks, such as hammerheads, are even scared away by bubbles produced by scuba divers. To follow sharks, scientists catch them and attach sonic tags to their fins. When the sharks are released, scientists can keep track of them by picking up radio signals with a receiver. Great care is taken to keep sharks alive when they are caught for tagging and other studies. Also, certain types of sharks are captured and placed in aquariums, where they can be easily observed (pp. 62–63).

HMS *CHALLENGER*
This British research vessel took 19th-century naturalists to the Atlantic, Pacific, and Indian oceans, where all kinds of marine life including sharks were collected.

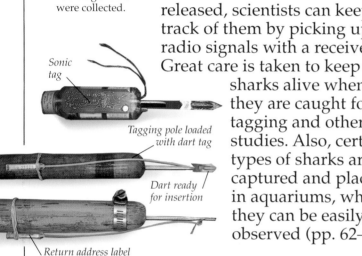

Sonic tag

Tagging pole loaded with dart tag

Dart ready for insertion

Return address label

Dr. John McCosker tracking sharks in Australia

Propeller measuring a shark's swimming speed is attached to fin of a mako shark

STUDYING LEMONS
Dr. Samuel Gruber has studied lemon sharks in the Bahamas for over 10 years. They do not mind being handled and do not need to swim to breathe, so they can be kept still while scientists make their observations. In this experiment (right), a substance is being injected into the shark to show how fast it grows. Young lemons, too, can have tiny tags inserted in their dorsal fins and are identified later by their own personal code number.

CHECKING UP A SHARK'S NOSE
American scientist Dr. Samuel Gruber checks the flow of water through this nurse shark's nose. Scientists have to be careful because, although nurse sharks are usually docile, they can give a nasty bite (pp. 18–19).

SCIENTISTS' FAVORITE
The lemon shark is one of the easiest sharks to study, both in aquariums and in the sea. A young lemon shark (left) attacks her food. When she eats, she shakes her head vigorously, scattering a large amount of debris in the aquarium's water.

TAGGING TIGERS
Scientists tag a small tiger shark in the Bahamas (top). Sometimes sharks need to be revived after this, so a diver (above) is pushing a large tiger shark along to keep water flowing over its gills.

KEEPING DRY
To go underwater without getting wet, Charles William Beebe (1877–1962) used this bathysphere in 1934 to reach a depth of 3,028 ft (923 m). Sharks as deep as 12,000 ft (3,600 m) are attracted by bait near the surface.

THE FRILL OF IT ALL
Three of these strange sharks (below) were caught off Japan in deep water during the 1870s *Challenger* expedition.

Frill shark

Sixth gill slit – most sharks have only five

Tagging sharks

SOME ANGLERS HELP SCIENTISTS find out where sharks go and how fast they grow by measuring, tagging, and releasing the sharks they catch. Tens of thousands of sharks have been tagged since the 1950s, off the coasts of Australia, the U.S., Africa, and the UK. A few tags are recovered when fishermen catch these sharks again. The record is for a male Australian tope, first tagged in 1951 and recaptured in 1986, 133 miles (214 km) from its original release site. It had grown by 7 in (17 cm). Blue sharks are among the greatest ocean travelers. One tagged near New York was caught 16 months later off Brazil, 3,700 miles (6,000 km) away; another tagged off the British coast was recaptured off Brazil, 4,350 miles (7,000 km) away.

Australian certificate (top) and card (bottom) for details of captured shark

Two Australian applicators with nylon and plastic tags

Tag

Metal pierc shark's sk

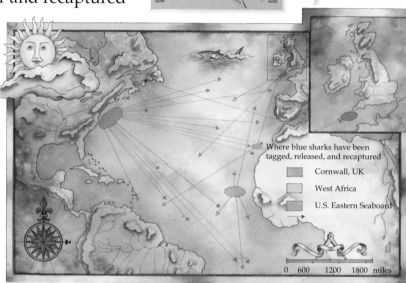

Where blue sharks have been tagged, released, and recaptured

- Cornwall, UK
- West Africa
- U.S. Eastern Seaboard

0   600   1200   1800   miles

BIRD RINGING
Ringing bands around young birds' legs gives information on migration – just as tags do for sharks – if they are caught again.

1 TAGGING/RELEASING SHARKS
Like most sharks, blue sharks have an excellent sense of smell and are attracted to boats by a dangling chum bag over the side containing smelly, salted fish. The chum's oil spreads out in a thin film over the water's surface, attracting sharks from a great distance. The shark hooks are baited with freshly caught mackerel, and the fishing lines are let out to depths of 40-60 ft (12–18 m).

Bait

2 HOOKED
Attracted by the oil and blood, the blue shark has taken the bait.

3 REELING IN
The shark is reeled in near the boat, very carefully, so as not to damage the shark.

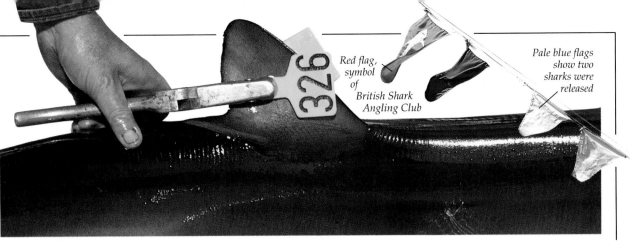

TAGGING
DORSAL FIN
[Th]e tag is made of [str]ong metal that will [not] corrode in seawater [and] cause the numbered [pla]stic tag to drop out. [On] the reverse side of [the] tag is an address [whe]re the tag can be [sen]t, should another [ang]ler or fisherman [cat]ch the tagged shark [aga]in in another part [of] the world.

Red flag, symbol of British Shark Angling Club

Pale blue flags show two sharks were released

7 RELEASING
Holding the shark by her tail, the skipper gently lowers her back into the sea. Once in the water, the shark swims away as fast as she can.

5 HOLDING THE SHARK DOWN
This female blue shark is 5 ft (1.5 m) long and weighs about 50 lb (22.5 kg). The skipper holds her down and gets ready to insert the tag. The shark can tolerate being out of the water for only a few minutes, so he has to work quickly to put the tag into her dorsal fin. Buckets of salt water are thrown onto the shark to help keep her alive. In other tagging studies, the shark is brought close to the boat but not landed, to avoid damaging it. Then a pole is used to stick the tag into the shark (pp. 28–29).

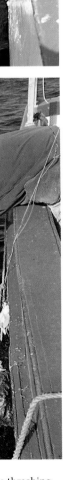

THRASHING SHARK
The skipper begins to haul the thrashing shark in, but it fights every bit of the way.

Shark overkill

PEOPLE KILL SHARKS for their meat, fins, skin, and liver oil, as well as for pure sport. Sport fishing can reduce the numbers of sharks found locally, but the biggest threat to sharks is overfishing worldwide. Sharks caught on long lines and in fishing nets are often thrown back into the sea dead, because it is other fish hauled in at the same time that are wanted. Sometimes just the shark's fins are removed and its body thrown back. Sharks are also killed each year in nets to protect swimmers. Sharks have a much slower rate of reproduction than bony fish and take a long time to mature. If too many are killed, their numbers may never recover. Efforts are now being made to protect sharks by creating reserves and restricting how many are caught.

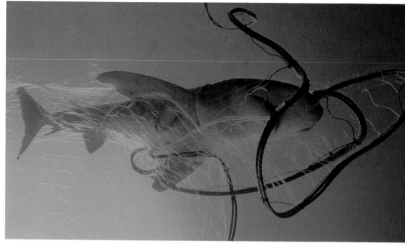

ANGLING
Angling (fishing with a hook and line) is a popular sport. Fast, strong sharks represent a big challenge. Today, angling clubs are becoming more aware of conservation, and some are restricting the size of shark that can be landed. Increasingly, anglers are encouraged to release sharks, instead of killing them (pp. 56–57).

WALLS OF DEATH
Drift nets (top), some 50 ft (15 m) deep and many miles long, are used to catch fish. The nets are so fine that fish do not see them and become trapped in the mesh. Sharks, like this oceanic whitetip shark (above), are easily caught, along with seabirds, turtles, and dolphins.

WHITE DEATH
For many anglers, the great white (above) is the ultimate trophy. People are frightened of great whites and so kill them, but as one of the sea's top predators, these sharks are important in keeping the natural balance in the ocean. The hunting of great whites is banned in South Africa. In Australia, these sharks are also protected.

SPORT OR SLAUGHTER
To show just how many sharks were killed, this hunter's boat (left) shows a collection of the victims' jaws.

Drift net

THRASHED THRESHER
Thresher sharks (left) are heavily fished in both the Pacific and Indian oceans. They are caught with long lines and gill nets. Landing a thresher can be dangerous, especially if they lash out with their tails; sometimes their tails get hooked on long lines.

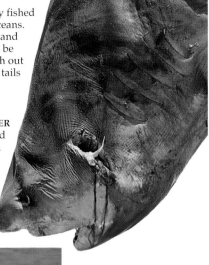

SAD END FOR A TIGER
This tiger shark (right) was killed in an angling competition in Florida. Near some coastal resorts, the numbers of large, predatory sharks – like the great white and tiger – have declined, probably because large numbers of them are still being caught by anglers.

ting up sharks for meat

FISHING FOR FOOD
In developing countries, people, like these Asians (left), depend on shark meat for protein. In other countries, shark is often a luxury food in restaurants. Whether we choose to eat shark or not, it is important that shark fishing is controlled. If not, these fascinating creatures could disappear from the world's oceans.

DRYING FINS
Shark fins are used in Chinese cooking for delicacies like shark-fin soup. Because the fins can be dried, they are much easier to market than shark meat, which has to be sold quickly or processed.

ark
s
ying

FINNING
These Japanese fishermen on a boat in the Pacific Ocean are cutting the fins off sharks caught in drift nets. They throw the rest of the shark back in the sea. Fins of many different kinds of sharks are removed, sometimes when the sharks are still alive. When thrown back in the sea, they take a long time to die. Without their fins, they are not able to swim properly and may be torn apart by other sharks.

Use and abuse

PEOPLE HAVE FOUND A USE for almost every part of a shark's body. The tough skin can be turned into leather, the teeth into jewelry, the jaws into souvenirs, the carcass into fertilizer, the fins into soup. The flesh can be eaten, and the oil from the liver may be used in industry, medicines, and cosmetics. Human exploitation of wild animals like sharks can cause a serious decline in their numbers, if more animals are killed than can be replaced by the birth and survival of the young. Sharks are especially at risk because they are slow to reproduce. It is hard to put sensible limits on the numbers of shark that can safely be fished because so little is known about them. Today, sharks are mainly exploited for their meat and fins, and demand for shark meat will probably continue as the human population increases. If fewer people were to use products derived from sharks, their future would be more secure. Otherwise, the effect on the natural balance in the oceans could prove to be disastrous.

NAPOLEON AND THE SHARK
Sailors feared and disliked sharks. Here, the French emperor Napoleon (1769–1821) watches a shark being killed, during his journey into exile on the remote Atlantic island of St. Helena.

SHARK TEETH
These pendants are made from the teeth of the great white shark. Some people mistakenly think that wearing shark tooth pendants make them look as fierce as a great white.

GETTING A GRIP
This sword handle, covered with rough sharkskin, gives a swordsman a secure grip.

In battle, a bloody handle could still be gripped

The sharkskin on the handle of this British Royal Artillery officer's sword has been dyed black

Rough rayskin under black cord

SAMURAI SWORD
This 19th-century sword once belonged to a samurai warrior from Japan. Its handle is covered with unpolished rayskin, and the sheath is made of the polished and lacquered skin of a ray (pp. 8–9).

Lacquered rayskin-covered sheath

Carved ivory handle

PERSIAN DAGGER
The sheath of this 19th-century Persian dagger is covered in rayskin. A flowery design has been painted onto the lacquered skin.

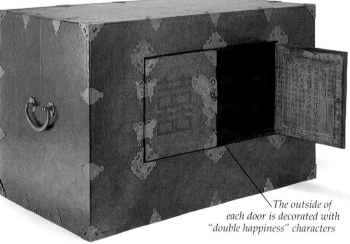

The outside of each door is decorated with "double happiness" characters

BOX OF HAPPINESS
Fine sharkskin, or leather, was used to cover this early 20th-century rectangular box from Korea. The leather is smooth because the denticles, or small teeth, have been highly polished, then lacquered, and dyed dark green. Shagreen – rough, unpolished sharkskin – is used as an abrasive, like sandpaper, for polishing wood.

SHARK REMAINS
These two hammer-heads (pp. 42–43) were caught off the coast of the Baja Peninsula in western Mexico. In this poor area, their meat was probably used for food and their skin for making into leather goods, such as wallets and belts.

JAWS FOR SALE
Many sharks are killed and their jaws sold to tourists as souvenirs. Jaws of large sharks, like the great white (pp. 28–31), fetch high prices. The sale of great white jaws is now banned in South Africa.

**SHARK
AND CHIPS**
Much of the fish
sold in British fish-
and-chip shops is, in fact,
spiny dogfish (pp. 22–23), one of
the most abundant and heavily fished
kinds of shark. Many kinds of shark are
given a different name when sold for
meat – dogfish is disguised as "rock
salmon" in Britain. In the past, people
did not like to eat shark because they
thought sharks ate the bodies of dead
sailors. Sadly, shark steaks are becoming
a fashionable delicacy in some restaurants.

**HEADLESS
CORPSE**
This shark was killed for sport
and had its head cut off so its
jaws could be removed. Shark
jaws are popular trophies in
the same way that hunters
show off the head and horns
of deer they have shot.

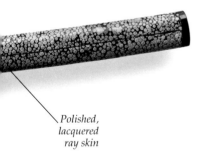

*Polished,
lacquered
ray skin*

SHARK LIVER OIL PILLS
In some countries people believe that shark oil can cure all
kinds of ills. Shark oil is composed of many different
substances, including vitamin A, but this
vitamin can now be made artificially.

A cluster of shark
liver oil pills

Two bowls
and a can of an
Asian delicacy –
shark-fin soup

SHARK-FIN SOUP
The cartilaginous fibers in
shark fins are made into soup,
which some Asian cultures regard as a
delicacy. The dried fins are soaked and
repeatedly boiled to extract the mass
of gelatinous fibers. Many other
ingredients are then added to
these noodle-like fibers to
give the soup some taste.

SKIN CARE
Shark oil is used in costly
skin creams that are meant to
prevent wrinkles and signs of
aging. But other creams, based on
natural plant oils, are just as effective.

Save the shark!

SHARKS HAVE A BAD reputation as blood-thirsty killers. But only a few kinds of sharks are dangerous (pp. 48–49) and attacks on people are rare. Other animals like tigers and even elephants, which also occasionally kill people, are more popular. Naturalists and other people are concerned because sharks are increasingly threatened by overfishing (pp. 58–59). Some sharks, like lemon sharks in Florida, also suffer because of the destruction of mangrove swamps, which are important nurseries for their pups. Many people begin to like and admire sharks as they learn more about them. In an aquarium, people can observe the grace and beauty of sharks. Good swimmers can learn to snorkel and scuba dive, and may be lucky enough to see sharks in the sea. In some areas, scuba divers are taken on trips to specific places where they can observe sharks in the wild.

MAD ABOUT SHARKS
This crazy sculpture of a blue shark on the roof of a house near Oxford, England, shows just how much some people like sharks.

Making sketches of various sharks in an aquarium

TANKS FOR THE VIEW
Seeing sharks come within inches of your nose is a great thrill, even if there is a glass wall in between (right). But not all kinds of sharks can be kept in aquariums. The fast-moving blue sharks and makos are used to roaming over great distances and need much more space than there is in an aquarium. A great white shark was once kept in an aquarium for a few days, but it became disoriented, continually hitting its nose against the glass, so it had to be released into the sea. Smaller sharks, like smoothhounds (pp. 14–15), are the easiest to keep in an aquarium.

Face to face with a shark (right) and feeding time at the aquarium (far right)

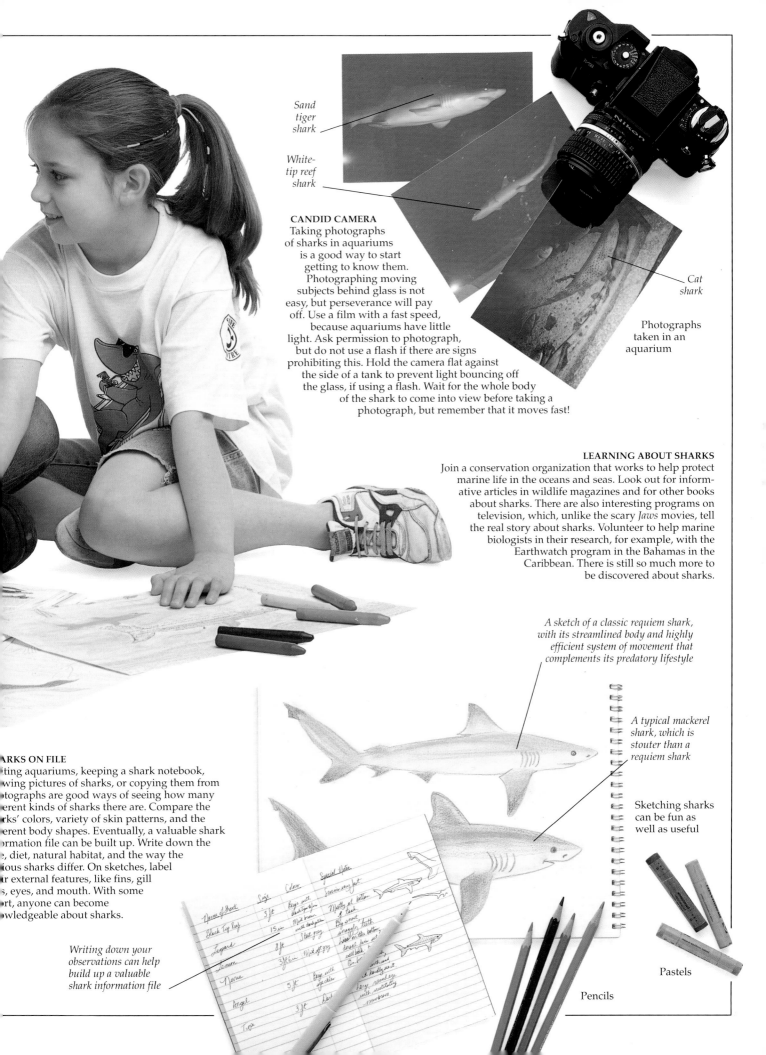

Sand tiger shark

White-tip reef shark

Cat shark

Photographs taken in an aquarium

CANDID CAMERA

Taking photographs of sharks in aquariums is a good way to start getting to know them. Photographing moving subjects behind glass is not easy, but perseverance will pay off. Use a film with a fast speed, because aquariums have little light. Ask permission to photograph, but do not use a flash if there are signs prohibiting this. Hold the camera flat against the side of a tank to prevent light bouncing off the glass, if using a flash. Wait for the whole body of the shark to come into view before taking a photograph, but remember that it moves fast!

LEARNING ABOUT SHARKS

Join a conservation organization that works to help protect marine life in the oceans and seas. Look out for informative articles in wildlife magazines and for other books about sharks. There are also interesting programs on television, which, unlike the scary *Jaws* movies, tell the real story about sharks. Volunteer to help marine biologists in their research, for example, with the Earthwatch program in the Bahamas in the Caribbean. There is still so much more to be discovered about sharks.

A sketch of a classic requiem shark, with its streamlined body and highly efficient system of movement that complements its predatory lifestyle

A typical mackerel shark, which is stouter than a requiem shark

Sketching sharks can be fun as well as useful

⌐ARKS ON FILE

⌐ting aquariums, keeping a shark notebook, ⌐wing pictures of sharks, or copying them from ⌐tographs are good ways of seeing how many ⌐erent kinds of sharks there are. Compare the ⌐rks' colors, variety of skin patterns, and the ⌐erent body shapes. Eventually, a valuable shark ⌐ormation file can be built up. Write down the ⌐e, diet, natural habitat, and the way the ⌐ious sharks differ. On sketches, label ⌐r external features, like fins, gill ⌐s, eyes, and mouth. With some ⌐rt, anyone can become ⌐wledgeable about sharks.

Writing down your observations can help build up a valuable shark information file

Pastels

Pencils

Index

Acknowledgments

Dorling Kindersley would like to thank:
Alan Hills, John Williams, and Mike Row of the British Museum, Harry Taylor and Tim Parmenter of the Natural History Museum, Michael Dent, and Michael Pitts (Hong Kong) for additional special photography. The staff of Sea Life Centres (UK), especially Robin James and Ed Speight (Weymouth) and Rod Haynes (Blackpool), David Bird (Poole Aquarium), and Ocean Park Aquarium (Hong Kong), for providing specimens for photography and species information.
The staff of the British Museum, Museum of Mankind, the Natural History Museum, especially Oliver Crimmen of the Fish Dept, the Marine Biological Association (UK), the Marine Conservation Society (UK), Sarah Fowler of the Nature Conservation Bureau (UK), the Sydney Aquarium (Darling Harbour, Australia), John West of the Aust. Shark Attack File (Taronga Zoo, Australia), George Burgess of the International Shark Attack File (Florida Museum of Natural History, USA), Dr. Peter Klimley (University of California, USA), and Rolf Williams for their research help.

Djutja Djutja Munuygurr, Djapu artist, 1983/1984, for bark painting. John Reynolds and the Ganesha (Cornwall) for the tagging sequence. Oliver Denton and Carly Nicolls as photographic models.
Peter Bailey, Katie Davis (Australia), Muffy Dodson (Hong Kong), Chris Howson, Earl Neish, Manisha Patel, and Helena Spiteri for their design and editorial assistance.
Jane Parker for the index.

Maps Sallie Alane Reason
Illustrations John Woodcock
Picture credits
t=top, b=bottom, c=center, l=left, r=right
Ardea: Jack Daniels 41tr; Mark Heiches 52bl; D Parer & E Parer-Cook 19tc; Peter Steyn 8b, 30bc; Ron & Valerie Taylor 7br, 18cl, 19tl, 25bc, 38bl, 40cl, 49ct, 52t, 52bc, 53tr, 53t, 53cr, 53br; Valerie Taylor 19bl, 31, 51c, 51bl, 60tr; Wardene Weisser 8c.
Aviation Picture Library/Austin J Brown: 35br.
The British Museum/Museum of Mankind: 46tl.
Bridgeman: The Prado (Madrid), The Tooth Extractor by Theodor Rombouts (1597-1637), 32bl; Private Collection, The Little Mermaid by E S Hardy, 21tl.
Capricorn Press Pty: 51t, 56tl, 56tr.
J Allan Cash: 27br, 50tr, 51tlb.
Bruce Coleman Ltd: 59c.
Neville Coleman's Underwater Geographic

Photo Agency: 20cr, 61cr.
Ben Cropp (Australia): 50ct, 50b.
C M Dixon: 47cr.
Dorling Kindersley: Colin Keates 25tr, 32br; Kim Taylor 21tl; Jerry Young, 9cr, 42cr.
Richard Ellis (USA): 17r.
Perry Gilbert (USA): 51tr, 51trb.
Peter Goadby (Australia): 28t.
Greenpeace: 58tr; 59br.
T Britt Griswold: 44b.
Tom Haight (USA): 45t.
Sonia Halliday & Laura Lushington: 50tl.
Robert Harding Picture Library: 18tr.
Edward S Hodgson (USA): 61bl.
Eric & David Hosking: 56cl.
The Hulton Picture Company: front cover ct, 34tl, 42cl.
Hunterian Museum (Glasgow): 13c.
The Image Bank/Guido Alberto Rossi: 30t.
Intervideo Television Clip Entertainment Group Ltd: 6t.
F Jack Jackson: 49cr, 49br.
C Scott Johnson (USA): 50cb.
Stéphane Korb (France): 58cr, 58b.
Frank Lane Picture Agency: 30br.
Eric Le Feuvre (USA): 20br.
William MacQuitty: 45bc.
Mary Evans Picture Library: front cover br, 10t, 36t, 38t, 40t, 48tl, 52tl, 55br, 60tl.
National Museum of Natural History, Smithsonian Institution (Washington, DC): Photo Chip Clark 13r.
NHPA: Joe B Blossom 23cr; John Shaw 23tl; ANT/Kelvin Aitken 48cr.
National Marine Fisheries Service: H Wes Pratt 54ct, 59tl; Greg Skomal 54bl; Charles Stillwell 23tc, 23tr.

Ocean Images: Rosemary Chastney 28b, 29c, 54cl; Walt Clayton 15br, 49cl; Al Giddings 15cr, 45br, 48cl, 49bl, 53bl; Charles Nicklin 29br; Doc White 20cl, 20_
Oxford Scientific Films: Fred Bavendam 25cl, 39b; Tony Crabtree 34b, 35t; Jack Dermid 25cr; Max Gibbs 27cbr; Rudie Kuiter 43bl; Godfrey Merlen 43br; Peter Parks 35c; Kim Westerskov 49tr; Norbert Wu 45cr.
Planet Earth Pictures: Richard Cook 59b_; Walter Deas 24bc, 39c, 48bl; Daniel W Gotshall 30cl; Jack Jackson 51br; Robert _ Jureit 22c, 22cr, 23c, 23cl; A Kerstitch 21cr 21bc, 21b; KenLucas 45br, 24cr, 39tr, 42bl_; Krov Menhuin 27bl; D Murrel 32t; Doug Perrine front cover bl, 22cl, 23br, 25t, 26b_ 54br, 55tr, 55cr; Christian Petron 42br; Brian Pitkin 24tl; Flip Schulke 30tl; Marty Snyderman 20bl, 27t, 42t, 43t, 54cr James P Watt 32t, 32b, 33t, 33b; Marc Webber 30bl; Norbert Wu 26c, 48b_
Courtesy of Sea Life Centres (UK): 62bl.
Shark Angling Club of Great Britain: 58c_
Courtesy of Sydney Aquarium (Darling Harbour, Australia): 62br.
Werner Forman Archive/Museum of Mankind: 47cl.
Courtesy of Wilkinson Sword: 60cl.
Rolf Williams: 16tl; 18cr (in block of six), 59tr, 61tr.

Every effort has been made to trace the copyright holders. Dorling Kindersley apologizes for any unintentional omissio_ and would be pleased, in such cases, to _ an acknowledgment in future editions.

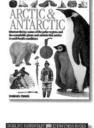

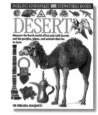

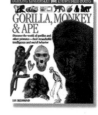